# MAYDAY!

# MAYDAY!

## ASKING FOR HELP IN TIMES OF NEED

### M. Nora Klaver

BERRETT-KOEHLER PUBLISHERS, INC.
San Francisco
*a BK Life book*

**Berrett-Koehler Publishers, Inc.**
235 Montgomery Street, Suite 650
San Francisco, CA 94104-2916
Tel: (415) 288-0260    Fax: (415) 362-2512   www.bkconnection.com

**Ordering Information**
*Quantity sales.* Special discounts are available on quantity purchases by corporations, associations, and others. For details, contact the "Special Sales Department" at the Berrett-Koehler address above.
*Individual sales.* Berrett-Koehler publications are available through most bookstores. They can also be ordered directly from Berrett-Koehler: Tel: (800) 929-2929; Fax: (802) 864-7626; www.bkconnection.com
*Orders for college textbook/course adoption use.* Please contact Berrett-Koehler: Tel: (800) 929-2929; Fax: (802) 864-7626.
*Orders by U.S. trade bookstores and wholesalers.* Please contact Ingram Publisher Services, Tel: (800) 509-4887; Fax: (800) 838-1149; E-mail: customer.service@ingrampublisherservices.com; or visit www.ingrampublisherservices.com/Ordering for details about electronic ordering.

Berrett-Koehler and the BK logo are registered trademarks of Berrett-Koehler Publishers, Inc.

Printed in the United States of America

Berrett-Koehler books are printed on long-lasting acid-free paper. When it is available, we choose paper that has been manufactured by environmentally responsible processes. These may include using trees grown in sustainable forests, incorporating recycled paper, minimizing chlorine in bleaching, or recycling the energy produced at the paper mill.

**Library of Congress Cataloging-in-Publication Data**
Klaver, M. Nora, 1959–
     Mayday! : asking for help in times of need / by M. Nora Klaver.
        p.    cm.
     Includes bibliographical references.
     ISBN 978-1-57675-451-1 (pbk. : alk. paper)
     1. Help-seeking behavior. I. Title.

HM1141.K53 2007
155.9′2—dc22
                                          2007010754

First Edition
12 11 10 09 08 07              10 9 8 7 6 5 4 3 2 1

Interior design: Detta Penna
Copyeditor: Pat Brewer
Indexer: Joan Dickey

*For Nanie and Bill,*
*I love you.*

# CONTENTS

# PREFACE

*Desire, ask, believe, receive.*
Stella Terrill Mann

## Stranger on a Plane

Just as you probably are, I am uncomfortable asking for help. A few years ago, however, when my personal life began falling apart, I was forced to seek the help I had avoided for so long.

In my late thirties, after several years of focusing intently on my career, I found myself single and almost completely isolated from other people. Somehow I had disconnected with my world and wasn't sure how to reestablish friendships and loving relationships. Fortunately I discovered how to reconnect and become more open and vulnerable.

I was encouraged by the insights of one of my teachers, Sonia Choquette, to become less relentlessly independent. Sonia is the author of several books, including *Your Heart's Desire*. Her advice made sense . . . but how does one go about becoming less independent?

Sonia's challenge to me was to ask for help three times a day, every day!

I remember sitting across from her, staring blankly and barely breathing. It wasn't that I was intimidated by the challenge; I was simply stumped as to when I might ever ask for help. After all, I was a help provider! My chosen vocation as an executive coach was all about rendering help to those who needed it. Outside of work, as well, I was often the first to give up my seat, to offer directions, to open doors. As I sat facing Sonia, my mind raced. Given the way I had structured my life—living alone and working alone most days—I couldn't identify many obvious opportunities to ask for help. It wasn't impossible, but it certainly wasn't easy.

Characteristically, I tackled all by myself the question of how to ask for help. It never even occurred to me that *I could ask someone* to help me identify opportunities to make requests for help!

I began with small steps. At a client site, I asked for instructions on how to set up voice mail. On another occasion, I asked for driving directions to a meeting, even though I already knew how to get there. I even asked a company president to buy me a can of soda when I was thirsty and didn't have any change for the machine. I was uncomfortable asking, but I didn't experience any real breakthroughs . . . until the end of a business trip.

I had spent the week coaching a number of challenging clients in another city. On Friday evening I found myself and my return flight delayed because of bad weather. Hours later the skies cleared, and we were allowed to board the plane.

Exhausted and impatient, I made my way to my seat. As I leaned down to release the handle of my rolling suitcase, it jammed. Acutely aware of the long line of other passengers behind me, I struggled with the handle, trying to force it down.

Here it was! A perfect opportunity for me to ask someone to lend a hand. All I had to do was turn around and make my request. I was fully aware of the voice in my head that demanded, *Ask for help!* If only I had. Instead, pride restrained me.

A man in line behind me noticed my efforts and offered to assist. Following my ingrained habits of self-sufficiency and blatantly ignoring the voice in my head, I remained as stubborn as the suitcase handle. Not even taking time to look this kind man in the eye, I shook my head and replied brusquely that I could take care of it myself. After a few more attempts, I finally slammed the handle home, viciously catching my thumb.

The man offered again, insisting that, really, he was happy to help. With my eyes averted and my injured thumb in my mouth, I shook my head again. I must really have looked ridiculous! Taking a deep breath, I bent down and tried to lift the case into an empty bin... but I just couldn't do it. My muscles seemed to have stopped working.

Needless to say, I was mortified. Mercifully, this man then saved me further embarrassment by simply taking the case from me and placing it neatly in the bin.

As I offered my thanks, I straightened up and finally looked him in the face. I noticed that he was smiling. In fact, his smile transformed me. At that moment I felt connected to this gentleman—not in a romantic, stranger-on-the-plane way, but simply as one person to another.

I finally understood the lesson. *Asking for help not only gets my needs met but, even more important, offers me a chance to be touched by another soul.*

After my self-inflicted humiliation on the plane, I began to take a more serious look at the process of asking for help. In that brief moment with a complete stranger, I realized that my life could be different, could be so much more than it was. I began to see possible connections everywhere, especially now that I had personally experienced at least one key benefit: emotional connection with another person.

## Before Desperation Sets In

Do you know the etymology of the word *mayday*? It comes from the French *m'aidez* (pronounced much like the English word *mayday*). It literally translates to "help me." Whenever we use the word or send out a *mayday* signal, that's literally what we mean: help me.

Mayday is the international call signal for distress used by ships and aircraft that are in the midst of the most severe circumstances. Because of this, the word *mayday* sometimes denotes hopelessness or desperation.

People tend to cry mayday when they've reached their own personal threshold of despair. Why wait until we hit that point of desperation? Why not see the word *mayday* as an *everyday* request for help? Why not cry mayday for the small things like help with the laundry or with a report that is due? It is possible. We can view the intimidating act of asking for help as a gesture of hope and optimism and not one of despair and misery.

There are a number of valid reasons why we don't ask for the help we need. It's important to know what stops us from doing what we know in our hearts is the right thing to do. So, that's where we'll begin: with why we don't ask for the help we deserve. Within Part One of the book, we'll explore why we don't ask, why we should, and the anchoring principles that make the *Mayday!* process work. *Try This* sections throughout the book are practical activities that will breathe life into the concepts and principles of the *Mayday!* process. You might want to set up a word-processing file where you can write your thoughts and comments on the Try This activities.

In Part Two of the book, you will discover the seven-step process that will change the way you see and, equally important, *perform* the act of asking for help. Designed to strengthen and clarify your requests, the *Mayday!* process will lead you to more profound friendships, greater intimacy, and a life of simplicity, ease, and flow. If, perhaps, you need to know the process right away, feel free to bypass Part One and dive right into the process beginning on page 75.

## The Language of Help

Just a quick word about the language of asking for help; English is somewhat limited in this regard. This may be because of our general discomfort in being reminded of our needs; the subject itself can be somewhat unpleasant. In particular, English has very few ways to refer to the person who agrees to our requests for help. "Helpmate," defined as a helpful companion or friend, is the word I've used most often.

Also, I have done my best to balance gender references. Men and women may not have the same specific needs, and they may not ask for assistance in the same way, but they do possess the same fears and cultural inhibitions. That said, examples are included from both men and women, and the pronouns *he* and *she* are both used throughout the book.

As a coach, I respect deeply the views of my clients. Some experience life through their fives senses: sight, smell, touch, hearing, and taste. Others are in tune with the metaphysical and spiritual—I refer to them as six-sensory individuals. I appreciate both the tangible and intangible and am pleased when my clients benefit from my insight. Yet, I am determined not to convert anyone. Regardless of belief and worldview, my job is to coach in a way that serves. I will never advise a spiritual person to "get real" nor will I push one belief system over any other. In coaching, I rely on what works, whether it is a practical tip or a spiritual practice. That said, this book is written for both five- and six-sensory individuals.

Pseudonyms have been used to protect the privacy of the people involved in each story. In some cases, elements of different situations have been combined to reinforce important concepts and principles.

Finally, *Mayday!* is not a traditional self-help book. In fact, its purpose is to motivate and guide as you move beyond the limits of *self*-help toward the unlimited potential found when you ask for help from *others*. Your personal lessons will increase if you have a specific issue or concern in mind. Then each lesson will shift from the realm of the theoretical to the practical. Even if you don't have a care in the world, you'll discover unvarnished stories from men and women—young and old, blue and white collar—who have had a few of their own. Many of these people didn't discover the process until they reached a point of desperation. This book is written to save you from that fate.

## Acknowledgments

As a new author, I have found the writing process to be equally exhilarating and intimidating. I've had to do my share of asking for help to make sure I have more of the former rather than the latter. As a result, I've been the recipient of many generous acts. I have a great deal to be thankful for.

I am deeply grateful for the wonderful people at Berrett-Koehler Publishers. My thanks to Johanna Vondeling for guiding me through this process with such care and understanding. And, my deep appreciation to Jeevan Sivasubramaniam, who responded so quickly and positively to the proposal that it took my breath away. He and Johanna were always there to lend supportive shoulders or wry comments. Thanks too, to Kristin Frantz and marketing team leaders Maria Jesus Aguilo and Catherine Lengronne. And special thanks go to Steve Piersanti who brought together all these talented people.

I am also very grateful to Sandra Reynolds, the first to really believe in the book. Thank you Karlin Sloan and Susan Spritz Myers, both insightful coaches and friends, who reviewed different sections of the manuscript. And, of course, great thanks to Andrea, Melissa, and my mother, Elaine and my father, William Klaver, who supported me the entire way.

I'd like to also thank my teachers: Don Grady, Terrie Lupberger, Julio Olalla, and Carolyn Myss. Your guidance and inspiration have led me down paths I never anticipated. Thank you.

Finally, I am indebted to those people whose stories appear in the book. Your hard-earned lessons have instructed me and will continue to teach others.

# PART 1

# THE
# MAYDAY!
## CALL

# GETTING READY

■ ■ ■ ━ ━ ━ ■ ■ ■

Complain to one who can help you.
*Yugoslav Proverb*

When was the last time you needed help? Yesterday? This morning? Or was it months ago? When was the last time you deliberately asked for help to meet your needs? Can you even remember? Was your request fraught with so much nervousness and discomfort that there is no possible way you'll ever forget the experience? Or did the appeal come naturally to you?

Strong, independent, and capable people blanch at the thought of asking for help. Each might benefit from the energies of others as they envision new lives, create new goals, embark on new careers, and implement new plans. Yet asking for help is the last action they will consider. No matter how strong we are, most of us work incredibly hard to avoid placing a simple call for help.

For many, asking for help is up there on the list of dreaded activities, right alongside the fear of public speaking or going to the dentist for a root canal. Asking for help can reveal our weaknesses and vulnerabilities. It can bring up unresolved issues of embarrassment and loss of control. It can test us like no other personal human challenge. Requesting help is so frightening that, even when faced with death, some of us will still not ask for that helping hand. There are those in the world who would, literally, rather die than let others know they are in need.

Yet, it's not usually life-threatening issues that we confront on a daily basis. Instead, we are consumed with smaller, imagined issues. Every day, no matter where you go, you may experience a need—a need for help. It may manifest at home, at work, at the park or grocery store. Need comes to us in many ways, degrees, and forms. It may be as simple as having someone help you carry a box, or as involved as having a friend help you move house. You may find yourself requiring a hand with the household chores or revealing a new perspective for your company strategy. Or perhaps your need is truly profound; perhaps you need extra care during a time of illness or recovery. Maybe you just need a financial boost to get yourself back on your feet again after a streak of bad luck. The act of asking for help enables us to satisfy our needs, large and small, profound and trivial. Rather than waiting for it to grow in size or in significance, why not ask for what we need when we need it?

If we do find a way to send out a mayday cry, we often do it badly. Possessed by anxiety, our words become hesitant, clumsy, and inarticulate. Instead of clear, strong, and centered mayday signals, we broadcast garbled ones, bathed in static. That static is our fear. With so much emotional "noise" your potential helpmate may remember your fear and not your request.

Making that request, not knowing whether your plea will be rejected, is bad enough. But actually having to relinquish control and let another care for us can be equally disturbing and uncomfortable. For many, *accepting* help can be devastating to their fragile egos.

Some see *asking* for help and *accepting it* as two completely different circumstances, but asking for and receiving help are closely aligned. The worries and concerns that prohibit us from doing either are exactly the same. One reason why some refuse to ask for help is because they know they'll have to accept it! Not only that, if we don't ask for help, it may be forced upon us. Trying to avoid making the request doesn't protect us from feeling that we will be viewed as weak, or that we will have to give up something in return for the help, or that we will lose something or someone if we take what is offered. Asking for help and accepting it go hand in hand.

## The Mayday! Process

There is a way to lessen your fears of asking and receiving help. It is called the *Mayday!* process. Composed of seven steps, this model will allow you to send out a different kind of mayday signal. Rather than one complicated by fear, *your call for help can be delivered from a position of strength, centeredness, and clarity of mind and heart.* The seven steps are:

### Before the Request

1. *Name the need:* Here you will learn about getting clear on your needs. You will also read about how important it

is to remain unattached to your first guess for resolving them.

2. *Give yourself a break:* This step asks you to apply the powerful emotional state of self-compassion to your situation. You will never be able to freely ask for help unless you believe you deserve it. This step helps you understand your personal worth and encourages you to ask for what you need.

## During the Request

3. *Take a leap:* This step supports you as you get ready to ask for that helping hand. Confidence that comes from faith is powerful enough to change your body as well as the words you use to form your request. With this vigorous emotional state in place, you will have the self-assurance necessary to take a leap of faith toward the help you seek.

4. *Ask!:* This step requires you to do it, to make the *ask*. The chapter that describes this step includes practical tips and suggestions for making your request a successful one.

## After the Request

5. *Be grateful:* Gratitude is a life-altering emotion. It changes how you view your circumstances. It shifts your focus toward your good fortune and away from what may be wrong. Gratitude allows you to remain gracious and open regardless of the answer to your request.

6. *Listen differently:* Once you've made your request, your only task is to listen carefully and completely to the response from your helper. This step explains why it is important to listen differently, not just to the words, but to the underlying emotional messages embedded in the response.

7. *Say thanks:* The final step of the *Mayday!* process is to say thank you—whether your helpmate agrees to help you or not. Say it, mean it, and say it again. Your helper will appreciate your gratitude.

Each step requires you to breathe deeply and consider both yourself and your helpmate. Awareness of yourself and others is essential to make this process work. In addition, the steps are more effective if you understand two anchoring principles. Both take advantage of the unappreciated power of our emotions. We have a tendency to ignore the emotional field, to dismiss our feelings. In doing so, we neglect to appreciate the ability of emotion to motivate us to act and to change our perceptions.

The anchoring principles will provide you with better insight into the concept of Applied Virtue. AVs are super emotions that will change you, your life, and your calls for help. Our fear wants us to believe one reality: that asking for help is too risky and not worth the energy. Applied virtue will show you a different reality: that the benefits of asking for help far outweigh the unlikely risks.

Application of these seven steps will lead you to experience a newfound stability and strength. They help you discover a sense of calm that will turn asking for help into a declaration of your value as a person, not just an acknowledgment of your frailty as a human being.

## The Forgotten Benefits of Asking for Help

Why should we bother asking for help if it is so much trouble and causes so much fear? There are benefits that we have forgotten, that have lain buried beneath our egos and our fear. Need blinds us to what is possible and present right now. The act of asking for help reveals what we cannot see.

The moment we decide to make a mayday call, we trigger a transformative energy that shifts us from the status quo into the realm of possibilities. We start on a journey toward a better future. When we ask for help, there is a greater chance that we will not be alone on that journey. Each request for help will serve as an invitation to share life for a while.

The act of asking for help is not only an invitation, it is a declaration, an assertion that we are deserving of assistance. When we venture to ask for what we need, we learn quickly that we are not alone and that there are resources, friends, and partners available to help. Asking for help can also re-introduce us to the beauty and inherent strength of gratitude.

Probably the most obvious reason for crying mayday is that we might just get help. This can lead to a life of greater simplicity and ease. You might even have a better chance at achieving "work/life balance," the holy grail of men and women everywhere who work and desire a life, too.

Reaching for that helping hand also stretches us beyond our current comfortable existence. It leads us into new and unexpected conversations and situations that test us and make us grow. Who knows what will happen when we present the question, "Will you help me?" We set in motion a series of events that few could have predicted. We automatically change our future from one of predictability to one of possibility.

More than anything, our mayday calls transform our

relationships by illuminating the emotions that lie just below the everyday surface stuff of life. Our requests create the potential for new connections where there once were none. At the same time, they can deepen existing bonds and even destroy others. It proves to us that we are deserving of help, that we are not alone, that we are already recipients of countless blessings.

## Getting Ready

You are about to embark on an emotional journey, a process that may challenge you in different ways. Decide now to be open to the activities, questions, concepts, and principles. Doing so will make your trip a bit smoother. The following visualization may help you get started.

If possible, spend the next few moments preparing yourself for this journey. Sit quietly in your chair. Pull your shoulders back, opening up your chest cavity, and breathe. Allow yourself to take at least three full breaths, holding each at the top until you feel your heartbeat. When your body wants your breathing to return to normal, let it.

Imagine that you are boarding a boat or ship of some kind. The destination is still unknown, but that doesn't concern you. You are ready for an adventure. Move forward to the bow of the boat and find a seat. Feel the soft lurch as the ship leaves the safety and familiarity of the dock. See before you a horizon of sunlight, sky, and blue waves. Feel the anticipation inside you as the boat moves ever forward.

Shift your attention to the lightly white-capped waves. They advance toward you ever so slowly. Each swell represents a lesson about asking for and accepting what you need. Instead of fearing them, feel curiosity about what it is they will bring to you. As you learn, you will ride, even surf, each wave. You will attempt to find your balance and keep your ship upright. You will also experience pleasant relief as your vessel survives the surge that accompanies each lesson. Some waves will be bigger than others, some will feel imperceptibly small. All of them have value to you.

Now breathe again, gently pulling yourself from this vision.

Asking for help is often our last resort, but it doesn't have to be. Your mayday calls don't have to be drowned out by desperation. Instead, they can be anchored in self-respect, confidence, and gratitude.

# CHAPTER 1

# WHY WE DON'T ASK

▮▮▮ ━ ━ ▮▮▮

*The significant problems we face cannot be solved at the same level of thinking we were at when we created them.*
*Albert Einstein*

Asking for help is a universally dreaded endeavor. We often choose instead to continue on alone, struggling valiantly and often unnecessarily with day-to-day burdens or even with crises, convinced that asking for help would exact an emotional price too high to bear. Nonetheless, in a world where people are living longer than ever before and may need ever more support over time, reliance on others has become increasingly necessary. It is time that the universal signal of mayday is sent.

No one is immune from need—not CEOs, not the cleaning staff, not store owners nor the store clerks. Grandparents, parents, and children all require a boost at some point. Team leaders and teammates, coaches and players, teachers and students, presidents and citizens all must, at some time, ask for aid.

Yet so many of us resist. One can't help but wonder, if we all experience need, why it is so hard to ask for another's help in satisfying that need. What parents wouldn't want their child to come to them with a problem needing resolution? What loving spouse wouldn't want to be called upon to support her partner? What leader would prefer to be kept in the dark if a team member needed help? There comes a time in everyone's life where we can't move forward unless we rely on others. The people who know and love us *want us to ask*. Yet we ignore our need. We pretend that we'll get through on our own, and in the process, deny the frail reality of our humanity.

Too many of us would rather go it alone when help is available . . . just for the asking. Something stops us from asking, but what, exactly, is it? A number of reasons are valid—to a point. What follows is an overview of the pressures that prevent us from asking for what we need. Each reason either muddies our mayday signals or stops us from sending them at all. When that happens, we lose more than we realize.

## We Were Never Taught How

Children are taught early to share their toys and treats. We regularly remind them—and ourselves—that it's right and polite to share with others. As self-involved little kids, we might hesitate to offer our toys and cookies, but after a while we see how pleased mom and dad look when we do. As we grow older, we begin to give generously because it feels good and not because it is expected.

Coming from a large family of nine children, I have early memories of "helping" around the house. We had our chores of course, but we were also expected to help one another, most of all the young ones. Regardless of how annoying my little brother could be, my duty was to hold his hand and guide him.

Sharing is important, no one argues that point. We may not notice, however, that as we teach our kids how to share, we inadvertently teach them other lessons as well.

When we encourage children to share, we acknowledge their position of abundance, whether it is a full plate of cookies or just more life experience. We also unintentionally point out that a difference exists between the two children: one has something, the other does not. A new, and uneven, power structure is established. The one blessed with abundance is usually the one with the power to decide what happens next. This unequal arrangement is fairly obvious to everyone involved; even the children may sense it.

Sharing is, and always will be, an important lesson to teach. But little time and energy have been spent advising us what to do when we are burdened with need or in a position of lack. Where are the lessons that teach us the best way to ask for what we need?

We encourage our kids to come to us when they need our help, or to seek out school counselors or trusted teachers. Encouragement is often where the lesson stops. Few of us explain how to ask, and fewer still describe why we should. No one learns to ride a bike on his own, and few people learn how to ask for help without someone to show them how.

The seemingly simple act of requesting help is more complex and less easily taught than our simple and frequent lessons on how to share. Thankfully, it is no less complicated than other lessons we learn along the way about personal honesty and integrity. Consider this book your new primer on how to make requests for what you need!

## We Have Few Models

We sometimes learn important lessons in life from stories containing models or archetypes. Classic tales like *Little Red Riding Hood* or *The Three Little Pigs* contain universal examples of acceptable and safe behavior. These archetypal stories and characters communicate images that are immediately recognizable and representative of the human condition. Passed down from generation to generation, they convey common and valuable truths.

Perhaps the greatest advocate of the wisdom of archetypes was Carl Jung, the renowned twentieth century psychologist. Jung examined archetypes extensively and theorized that they represent not only recognizable images, but also a shared human psyche. "The collective unconscious—so far as we can say anything at all about it—appears to consist of mythological motifs or primordial images, for which reason the myths of all nations are its real exponents. In fact, the whole of mythology could be taken as a sort of projection of the collective unconscious." If true, then archetypes instruct us at a very basic level about our own humanity.

Another of my teachers, Caroline Myss, author of the remarkable best seller *Sacred Contracts,* uses archetypes to illuminate the personal journeys we all take. A convenient and helpful *Gallery of Archetypes* is included at the end of *Sacred Contracts.* From Addict to Warrior, Myss describes seventy of the more common archetypal personas that humans adopt. You have already lived many of these: Child, Artist, Athlete, Companion, Lover, Saboteur, Victim, and Warrior.

From Myss and Jung we learn that archetypes contain familiar stories that don't just represent what we have in common; they also teach us great lessons about heroism, failure, and everyday existence. Was there an archetype that would teach us how to be vulnerable and still survive—how to ask for help? I began to search for a unifying and recognizable image that depicted a healthy approach to asking for help.

Those who ask for help are often seen as personifying the archetype of the Beggar. Caroline Myss describes it well; "Completely without material resources, the Beggar is associated with dependence on the kindness of others, living on the streets, starvation, and disease, whether in New York City or Calcutta." Clearly, the Beggar is not an image we usually want to emulate as we transmit our own mayday calls.

Or is it? Myss goes on to describe the Beggar in all of us; "People 'beg' for attention, love, authority, and material objects . . . From a symbolic perspective, the Beggar archetype represents a test that compels a person to confront self-empowerment beginning at the base level of physical survival. Learning about the nature of generosity, compassion, and self-esteem are fundamental to this archetypal pattern." When we ask for assistance, we do learn a great deal about generosity and the impact it has on our self-images. But these lessons are *indirect* consequences that come from acting out the Beggar archetype. The Beggar does not *directly* teach us how to ask for the help we need.

Perhaps ancient Greek mythology is able to provide a direct and positive model to show us how to ask for help. One story, in particular, seemed to demand a request for help, that of Demeter, the Goddess of the Earth, and her daughter, the beautiful Persephone. Ruthlessly kidnapped by Hades, the God of the Underworld, Persephone is separated from her mother. Realizing her beloved girl is gone, Demeter begins a frantic search that lasts for days. She finally goes to Zeus, her brother, and demands that he tell her where her daughter is. He refuses and Demeter in retaliation and grief, essentially, goes on strike, causing the fields of the Earth to lie barren and the rivers to dry up.

After reading a number of variations of the story, I wanted to shake Demeter's mythological shoulders and yell, "You fool! Why? Why didn't you just ask for help?" How could Demeter not know that people do not respond well to demands, especially mythological gods?

Another archetypal story is that of the Good Samaritan. The Bible tells of a man, brutally robbed and left for dead by the side of a road, who is helped by a stranger—a citizen of

Samaria. (For a sharply witty and thought-provoking study of this parable, read *Help: The Original Human Dilemma* by Garret Keizer.) As inspiring a story as this is, the Good Samaritan allegory contains lessons about giving help, not asking for it.

The Bible contains a number of instances of people beseeching God and Jesus for help. Some of the requests for help are implied, as in the story of Lazarus who was raised from the dead. Martha, Lazarus' sister, came to Jesus to inform him that her brother had died, but she did not directly request Jesus' intervention. Other stories, as well, have clear and straightforward pleas for help. In Mark 5:21, Jairus said to Jesus, "My little daughter is critically ill. Please come and lay your hands on her so that she may get well and live." And in Mark 7:24 a Canaanite woman approached Christ and "began to beg him to expel the demon from her daughter." In both cases, Jesus responds with compassion and healing.

Finally! Positive examples of requests for help! Jairus and the Canaanite woman both demonstrate that heartfelt pleas can be made and answered!

As affirming as these tales are, they still don't seem to fit as unifying and easily recognizable images. Quick! What comes to mind when you hear the word Beggar? More than likely you get an immediate image of a bedraggled person. Use the word in conversation and the other person will immediately understand your meaning. Now describe what comes to mind when you hear the words Jairus or Canaanite woman. More likely, your mental response is a blank one. How interesting that these affirming models have not made it into our cultural lexicon, while the negative model of Beggar has. Sadly, there seems to be no universally accepted and immediately familiar image that represents a person blessed with enough self-care to respectfully and clearly ask for what he or she needs.

In a workshop examining the three feminine archetypes, Virgin, Mother and Crone, I approached Jean Shinoda Bolen, Ph.D. and author of *Goddesses in Everywoman* and *Gods in Everyman*. We discussed my search for relevant archetypes. After some thought, Dr. Shinoda Bolen shook her head. "I'm not aware of any archetypes that support asking for help . . . but," she added, "If we don't have the model, we sometimes need to create our own." What an inspiring perspective! Perhaps one day, we will all serve as models for those who desperately need and want to ask for help.

## We Love Our Independence

Contemporary society has its own share of archetypes and models that dissuade us from asking for help. The iconic images of the United States celebrate the independent ideal: the lone cowboy, the business magnate who succeeds because of his own strong will and refusal to quit, and most recently, the super mom who raises her kids and simultaneously seals the multimillion-dollar deal. The classic American archetype is one who finds his own path and succeeds: Bill Gates, Thomas Edison, and Henry Ford. In film, we celebrate the power of the individual through characters played by strong, self-determining actors like John Wayne, Bette Davis, Katharine Hepburn, and Orson Welles. As a nation and a culture, we've been living with and promoting the dream of independence since 1776. Perhaps we've gone a bit overboard.

An offshoot of our love of independence is the value we place on the individual. In his work on defining national cultures, social scientist Geert Hofstede identified five key dimensions, one of which assesses a nation's tendency toward individualism or collectivism. Hofstede writes, "On the individualist side we find societies in which the ties between individuals are loose: everyone is expected to look after him/

herself and his/her immediate family. On the collectivist side, we find societies in which people from birth onwards are integrated into strong, cohesive in-groups, often extended families (with uncles, aunts and grandparents) which continue protecting them in exchange for unquestioning loyalty." Not surprisingly, the United States outranks all other nations—by a wide margin—on measures of individualization. One person, one vote; MySpace pages; personal playlists; personalized marketing, and the rise of the small, independent business owner—each is a testament to how much we value the individual.

Independence and individualization generate great stories of self-determination, but they can also lead to very lonely and isolated lives. Robert Putnam, author of the revealing *Bowling Alone,* cites startling statistics that bring to light the consequences of a culture driven by a relentless search for independence and personal self-expression. According to Putnam, in the last twenty-five years social capital, or the "ways in which our lives are made more productive by social ties" has dwindled. Attendance at club meetings is down 58%, involvement in church activities has dropped anywhere from 25 to 50%, and simply having friends over to the house has decreased by 45%. According to the December 4, 2006 issue of *Time Magazine,* "the number we count among our closest friends—the ones with whom we discuss important maters—shrank over the past 20 years, from three friends to two. At the same time, the number of Americans who have no one at all to confide in more than doubled, to 1 in 4." Troubling statistics that make asking for help more unlikely.

We have pulled away from one another. We have left behind many of the support systems that we once relied upon. This gradual separation from the whole contributes to and reinforces our natural reticence to ask for help. If we don't feel part of something or connected to others, then we reduce the number of potential helpmates. Stepping off society's dance floor keeps us believing we are alone, that no one is there to dance with us. Haven't we had enough of being alone and pulling ourselves up by our individual bootstraps? Have we gone too far with our infatuation with personal independence? Aren't we ready to get involved with each other again?

## We Don't Think To Ask

Brainwashed by the lure of independence and individualization, many of us have created singular lives that are grounded in self-sufficiency. So caught up in the habit of taking care of ourselves, we lose sight of when we might even need help!

Pam was, by all conventional measures, successful. She had an important position in her company and lived in an exclusive neighborhood in the city, but she was lonely and feeling the weariness of doing everything on her own. I offered her an assignment that had been given to me years before: Ask for help three times a day.

Pam couldn't do it. She struggled each day to come up with opportunities that would require her to ask for help. After a while, she forgot all about it. She slipped back into her routine of handling everything on her own.

Like Pam, many of us have become so habitually self-sufficient and compulsively busy that we have driven out all thoughts of asking for help. We have created lives that can be handled, for the most part, by one or two people. We'll never invite another in to help if we have become inured or oblivious to our needs.

## It's Easier to Do it Myself

Making a request for help is often hard. Asking for help requires a level of emotional risk and some are just not ready to take it on. For them, it is easier to find a way to soldier forward without assistance. Even if the emotional hurdles are overcome, accepting help might be more troublesome. Involving someone else would be more work/trouble/agony/aggravation/effort (take your pick) than it's worth.

Rudy, a somewhat successful artisan glass blower, found it too difficult to ask for help around the studio. He began working with glass when he was in college in the late '60s. He found he loved the creative process and over the years developed a signature style. There were times when he was so busy creating beautiful works of art and managing his small studio that he would have appreciated help, but Rudy just couldn't bring himself to ask. "It's not me," he told me once. It was easier for him to limit his time in the shop and get to the bookkeeping when he could.

During busy periods, when his glass was in demand, Rudy made the decision to work longer hours and to "be more efficient." Essentially, the emotional risk of asking for help caused Rudy more stress than working harder and longer. It was the trade-off he was willing to make. He's not alone. Every day, many of us decide that it's easier to handle it all ourselves rather than ask anyone else to help.

Rudy traded more than he realized. Working longer hours and trying to be more "efficient" took a toll on him. He was always unhappy and stressed during these peak periods. He would become resentful and impatient. He would pull away from his family. He never seemed to be available for important outings and events. Rudy never figured out how to get more done in less time. His strength was in blowing glass, not in balancing the books. If he had braved his fears and asked for what he needed, office help, he would have been free to create and to be with his family more.

Then there was Elaine, who ran a small restaurant. She resisted asking her staff to learn how to handle inventory and ordering, telling herself that it would take up too much time and that there would be too many mistakes made along the way that would cost her money. Elaine couldn't see what she was really giving up by doing it all herself. Her staff didn't hang around long. They would work for a few months and then leave for better jobs at other restaurants that offered them more opportunity to develop their skills. The ones that did stick around weren't the most motivated employees. They came, did their jobs, and left. After a while, Elaine found herself overworked with an unwilling staff.

Refusing to ask for what we need can be shortsighted and limiting. Sometimes asking another for help does create more problems than it resolves, but our assumption that it will play out that way is not always correct. We won't know until we make the request. Refusing to ask because we cannot control the end result does nothing more than imprison us in the way we've always done things. Choosing to go it alone can prevent us from using our energy in activities that inspire and ignite our imaginations.

## We're So Bad at It

Let's recap for a moment. *If* we do realize we need help, *and* we've never been taught how to ask for it *and* we've never really seen a good example *and* we have been discouraged by society, that would probably mean we are pretty bad at performing it. At the risk of sounding vulgar—no wonder we suck at asking for help.

Any teacher or corporate trainer will tell you that the way to develop a skill is to marry step-by-step instruction with a successful demonstration and then follow it up with practice. Until now, we've had no formal instruction on how to askfor help, and what we've seen and experienced are probably really bad examples. We've had our share of humiliating attempts. So we stumble on alone, convinced we just need to think it through some more. Avoidance, denial, and delusion rarely work, and they certainly don't lead to success when we have a need to meet.

If we are finally forced to ask—and this is usually when we've hit a point of desperation—our requests stink of that same despondency. We mess up our requests. Our mayday signals become garbled. If we go to the trouble of asking for help, we want to make absolutely certain that our requests are heard and understood. The less confusion we create when we ask for what we need, the better for us and for those who agree to help.

From experience, we know many things can go wrong if we make poor requests for help. Some consequences are embarrassing, all are miserably unpleasant. Here are some common ones:

♦ We may ask too late because we don't recognize early enough that we actually have a need to be filled.

♦ We may not see the whole picture, so the help we ask for satisfies only part of our need.

♦ We may ask the wrong person or people to help us with our request.

♦ Our requests may be so unclear that others may not understand that we need help at all.

♦ Help may come, but because we weren't clear enough in our requests, it's the wrong help.

♦ We may demand assistance rather than politely ask for it.

♦ We may resort to blackmail, bribery, or even coercion to get our needs met.

- We may inadvertently solicit pity instead of help.

- Our bodies may betray our fears and subtly send the message that we are too far gone to be helped.

- We may ask for help too often without concern for our friends, family and co-workers. Compassion fatigue becomes a real possibility for them.

- We may simply frighten ourselves into never asking.

Like any skill, practice is required. The more often you ask, the more comfortable you will become. With time, miscommunications will be reduced, anxiety will lessen, and your words will become more eloquent.

## The Law of Reciprocity

You may have never heard of the Law of Reciprocity, but you have adhered to it most of your life. It means to give and take mutually; an exchange of one favor or action for another of equal value. This rarely discussed, but general rule obliges us when we are on the receiving end of a generous act of help.

When we hear the following expressions, we know the Law of Reciprocity is at work: Treat others as you would yourself; Quid pro quo; Scratch my back and I'll scratch yours; Tit-for-tat; and Give-and-take. Even the concept of Karma, which states that the energy you put out into the Universe will return to you, is another manifestation of this law. When we find ourselves in a situation where we need aid, the Law of Reciprocity comes into immediate effect. Almost instantaneously, we wonder, "If she agrees, how can I ever pay her back?"

The Law of Reciprocity also prevents us from abusing our relationships by asking for help too often. It forces us to pause before we make our requests, giving us a moment to consider others and their needs. This universal rule is of great value, yet we can temper our use of it. Applied without care, the Law of Reciprocity could make our lives one tit-for-tat transaction after another. You do for me and I'll do for you. How cold! How mechanized! Adhering strictly to this law, would we begin tallying debits of need and credits of support?

My very good friend Vivian and I decided to drop this transactional way of assisting one another. We came to this decision during a shared vacation. On a trip to Ireland, I decided to arrange for top-drawer hotel accommodations for Vivian and myself. I thought that it would be a lovely way to experience the famous Irish hospitality and to pamper ourselves for a day or so. Over champagne that first afternoon, Viv confessed she was having a hard time figuring out how to pay me back for my generosity. I shook my head, laughed, and told her that some gifts are simply just gifts. They are not to be "paid back." For Vivian, this was a new way of looking at how we could care for one other and keep our friendship alive. We agreed from that point forward that we would learn to give without expectation of a return. This has naturally extended to how we help each other as well. When one of us needs something, we no longer worry about the cost of the assistance. We trust that our friendly give-and-take will balance in the long run.

Indeed, some acts of assistance are far too great to pay back, such as saving a life or providing care during a time of great illness. Who could even begin to think about repaying our parents for the guidance, love, and aid they've given us over the years? Placing a value on these selfless gifts is impossible. On a day-to-day basis however, our requests for help are not usually so great and overwhelming. Even if the Law of Reciprocity kicks in, you have the power to make a deliberate decision to override it. You can give yourself permission to ask for what you need.

## Fear

We have many reasons why we don't ask for the leg up or the helping hand—all valid. But at their core, each reason is an acceptable way of explaining the *fear* we feel about asking for help. Of course, you might not use the word *fear*. Instead, you might find yourself feeling *concerned* or *anxious*. Regardless of the semantics, some degree of fear holds you back from broadcasting your mayday signals. In its not so subtle way, fear tells you that asking for help is wrong, that you'll suffer more if you ask. Don't believe it. In the next chapter, we'll expose fear for what it is and reveal the hidden truths that it doesn't want you to hear.

### TRY THIS   WHAT STOPS YOU FROM ASKING?

Writing your responses serves to reinforce your own personal learning. Every **Try This** question and activity is available online at www .maydaythebook.com. I invite you to access the site to record your answers, thoughts, and musings.

- How far has your love of independence gone? What have you gained from being self-sufficient? What have you lost?

- When do you find it's easier to "do it myself?" How does that decision affect you in the short term? In the long run? How else could you spend your energy?

- In thinking of your failed requests for help, what went wrong? Refer to the lists in Step 6 for possible answers to this question.

- How have you "paid back" someone for his/her help? When did you not ask because the emotional or financial price seemed too high?

# CHAPTER 2

# WHY WE DON'T ASK—REALLY

■■■━━━■■■

Nothing in life is to be feared, it is only to be understood.
Now is the time to understand more, so that we may fear less.
*Marie Curie*

We do not ask for help because we are afraid. Fear is what stops us from looking someone in the eye, admitting a need, and saying the words, "I need your help."

Anthropologists describe fear as a natural, protective response to potentially dangerous stimuli. Fear kept our ancestors from venturing into caves populated by people-eating lions. Nowadays, it keeps us from venturing into equally dangerous dark alleys. This protective quality of fear is instinctual. The little hairs stand up on our necks and our eyes widen in anticipation of the risk ahead. This primal fear keeps us safe from harm and protects us from the very real and imminent perils that lie ahead.

We have come far from those days of the cave. For most of us, primal fear lies dormant. *Metus gravis,* or grave fear, is relatively rare. Living lives of comparative safety, few of us experience the cringing terror that accompanies urgent life or death situations. When we do, we rarely think twice about asking—no, screaming—for the help we need. Our instincts kick in and we react immediately to save ourselves. In those situations, the dread of asking for help usually pales in comparison to the heavy fear we feel if our lives are in danger.

If we are lucky, we may never have to experience this grave, primal fear. Daily, however, we go through fear of a different kind. This fear is of a lesser nature, and it keeps us quiet when we really want help the most.

What we feel more often is *metus levis,* or trifling fear. Taking the form of anxiety, concern, worry, and doubt, these ordinary fears do not arise from dangerous circumstances. Instead, they are generated by smaller, imagined threats that have little chance of coming true. These minor fears have little basis in reality, yet we latch on to them as though they were lifelines. Believing the odds to be greater than is actually probable, we accept the imagined threats as realities. Confusing fear with reality is a mistake. A helpful reminder is that FEAR can also be read as Fantasy Expressed As Reality.

Trifling fear can move us to resort to nasty measures to get what we want. Coercion, guilt, bribery, and blackmail are perversions of healthy and respectful mayday calls. Forcing others to help us through either emotional or physical pressure is not only unfair and unethical, it can also be illegal.

Instinctual fear, *metus gravis*, is necessary for our survival. Trifling fear is not. Trifling fear keeps us safe within our comfort zones. At the same time, it keeps us away from living the lives we always dreamed of. The *Mayday!* process addresses these trivial fears that get in our way, that stop us from asking for and getting the help we need.

Trifling fear is a liar. It takes a seed of truth and wraps it in falsehood. Then the lie is repeated inside our heads until we are, quite simply, brainwashed. Our intellect reasons that if the kernel is true, then the rest must be equally true, right?

Wrong. This little fear is the voice of the ego, that part of ourselves that Jung defined as the conscious mind. (From this point on, when I refer to fear, I mean trifling fear unless otherwise noted.) The conscious mind creates an image of how we would like to be: our persona. It works diligently to protect that facade. Yet, if the ego-driven persona is threatened in any way, trifling fear jumps into action. Motivated by self-preservation, this little fear makes a home for itself in our heads and whispers, screams, cajoles, and berates us until we believe its lies and give in.

## The Three Riptides of Fear

The sages say that the greatest fear of all is that of death. Three trifling fears appear, for some, no less frightening: Fear of Surrender, Fear of Shame, and Fear of Separation. These fears are like deceptive riptides that pull us away from the help that is waiting on shore. A riptide, or more accurately a rip current, is a powerful stream of water that pulls us seaward. They are difficult to spot since, on the surface, the water may appear calm, even placid. The riptides of the fears of surrender, shame, and separation act in the same way. They seduce us by telling us they only intend to keep us safe, yet following them can leave us alone and floundering. Exploring and understanding these dangerous currents will lessen their power over us and make our mayday calls substantially more effective.

## The First Riptide: The Fear of Surrender

Dr. Ahmad put down his scope and reached over to touch the hand of one of his elderly patients. He had just informed her of the diagnosis—cataract of the eye—and she was visibly shaken, terrified by the prospect of surgery. After reassuring her that the procedure was routine and that she'd be in great hands with the hospital staff, Dr. Ahmad asked her why she had taken so long to come in and see him about her weakening eyesight.

"Well," she replied, quickly forgetting her fear and replacing it with indignation, "I couldn't very well have asked my children to drive me! Otherwise they'd think I couldn't take care of myself, and then they'd have me in some old folk's home in no time!"

Dr. Ahmad shook his head as he told me this story. "There are so many like her. A lot of my older patients won't ask for the help they need. They wait too long for treatment. They are afraid of losing their independence and being at the mercy of someone else."

Dr. Ahmad had just offered a perfect example of the fear of surrender. Anytime we worry that we are about to lose our self-determination, independence, and control, we become victims of this riptide.

Just when we realize that something is not quite right, just as we begin to consider the possibility of asking for help, the riptide of surrender exerts its power. It seduces, like an eddy of calm water. Stepping into the sea, we believe we are safe. Then the riptide offers up a truth: Some control is good. We agree, remembering how satisfying it feels to be in control of our own lives. Then this dangerous current begins to swirl lies around us. It tells us that if *some* control is good, then *all* control must be good, and letting go of it is a terrible thing. This sounds right, so we move deeper into the sea. Then this deceitful current lies again, convincing us that asking for help will mean a loss of power. At this point, the riptide has us in its grip. We accept its lies. We believe that asking for help will surely leave us powerless and without control. And for many, the loss of power and control is just too frightening to risk or even contemplate.

Asking for help and accepting it requires us to surrender to at least one of three scenarios. We may have to relinquish control, or step blindly into an uncertain future, or even pay a price for what we need. In all three scenarios, surrender is an essential element for successful requests for help.

In order to meet a need, we may have to relinquish control. Whenever you say to yourself, "If I ask for help, she might want to solve my problem her way," or even, "Getting someone else to help me might mean that the job won't be done as well as what I would like," then you are caught in the riptide of the fear of surrender. You fear a loss of control.

Simple things like asking your spouse to fold the towels can turn into a battle of wills. If you prefer the towels folded in thirds and he likes them folded in half, then you may just have to surrender your power over the linen closet—especially if you really need the help. Everyone likes to have things done their way and if we truly need help, we may just have to relinquish our hold over such things.

Surrender may also mean stepping into an uncertain future. Referred to as the fear of the unknown, this is a misnomer. What we really fear is surrender to a future we cannot predict. If I hear myself say, "I don't know what will happen if I ask for help and that's what scares me," then I know I have succumbed to the riptide of the fear of surrender.

Surrender may also demand that we submit to paying a price for the assistance we receive. The thought of asking for help and potentially surrendering to another's price for that help can initiate terrible anxiety and fear. We may say to ourselves, "Whatever she might want in return is more than I could bear to pay." This, of course, is the classic fear of petitioners of Mafia dons the world over. Thankfully, most of us keep our interactions with organized crime to a minimum. Still, a perfectly legal favor may have to be repaid and the price may remain unknown until the chit is called in.

The cost of help can also be exacted in actual dollars and cents. Jamal feared asking for assistance because he thought it might lead to a loss of financial stability, something he had worked hard to acquire. He was concerned that he would lose a substantial sum of his own savings if he requested help in starting a small business. Ultimately, it's not the loss of money he feared. What triggered his anxiety was the thought of surrendering to a new set of (self-imposed) restrictions in his personal and professional life. Jamal's fear of surrender flashed vivid images of destitution and poverty as it attempted to convince him that going it alone was better than succumbing to the price of asking for help. The potential loss of money can be devastating to all of us, yet money itself is a means to an end. Surrendering to the consequences of not having money is what really terrifies us.

## The Love of Control

The fear of surrender would have no power over us if we didn't care about control. That desire to control ourselves, others, and circumstances makes this riptide so powerful. Without realizing it, we judge that we know better than anyone else how life should be. In reality, when we refuse to surrender, we cut ourselves off from possibilities that we cannot even begin to imagine.

We experience a misleading rush of power when (we think) we've made something happen, as though we were minor gods in the heavens. In our hubris we reject the idea (even though we understand this intellectually) that *control is impossible*. At the very most, we may be able to exert control over ourselves. Even then, self-control is often no more than a wish.

In *Out of Africa,* a gorgeous film (based on the book of the same name) depicts author Karen Blixen's gradual release of control during her years spent in Kenya. Near the end of the film, Meryl Streep's character sighs wearily after losing a battle to hold back a nearby river and prevent it from flooding her coffee plantation. "This river lives in Mbassa," she says. "It wants to go home." The river teaches her the futility of control. From this scene on, she accepts what she has been fighting against: the flow of life.

*Contra*, the linguistic root of the word *control*, means "against." When we seek to control, like Karen Blixen did, we work against what is.

I have my own lessons about control to contribute. Years ago I was diagnosed with a benign tumor that was growing too near an important nerve. Surgery was required, and I listened intently as the surgeon explained the procedure and the postoperative process. When he said that I'd be incapacitated for a week, tears filled my eyes. I wasn't worried about the surgery. No, I knew what to expect. I was more concerned about actually having to ask someone for help.

Noticing my tears, the doctor reached out to touch my hand. "Are you okay?" he asked. I stifled a sob and cried, "Who will stay with me? I have no one to help me."

I had worked for years to create a persona of a confident and capable professional woman. I didn't need much from other people. Over the years it had become increasingly uncomfortable for me to rely on anyone at all. My ego stated flatly that a strong, independent woman wouldn't find herself in this kind of situation. It was as though this tough persona of mine was just begging for a lesson in humility and surrender.

Later that day I called my then-boyfriend, Robbie, and told him I needed both surgery and his help. Notice that I didn't ask him; I *informed* him I needed help. He reluctantly agreed to stay with me for a week after the operation. I heard the hesitation and reluctance in his voice, but I stubbornly focused on his agreement to be there for me.

I should have listened more closely to what he was telling me, or rather, not telling me. Two days before the surgery, Robbie dumped me.

I had no choice. I was forced to call upon those my ego swore I would never rely upon again: my parents.

Don't get me wrong, my relationship with my folks was good, but I was still seduced by my independent self-image. My ego voice whispered that giving in to their care would erase all the hard work I had done in creating such an impressively independent (albeit lonesome) life. I hated the thought of asking because, in a very real way, it meant I couldn't handle my life by myself. Accepting help wasn't easy either. It drove me mad to think that I would have to surrender to my parents' care after all these years.

I am heartily ashamed to say that I was blatantly ungracious as I made the call to my mother. First, I sobbed about my breakup and then I asked her if she would care for me. She agreed immediately, but my fear of surrender wouldn't allow me to end the call with an appreciative and grateful tone. Instead, I warned her, "I don't want you and dad fussing over me! I am not a child, and I don't expect to be treated like one!"

That's exactly what I was, of course; a frightened, ungrateful child. In my feeble and awkward way, I was still trying to control the situation. The lesson didn't hit home until I woke at 2:00 AM to find my mother sleeping in the hospital room. I was deeply touched by the sight of her, curled uncomfortably in a chair. Unable to move or speak, with no strength to control anything, I realized I had no choice but to let go. I no longer cared about being successful or independent. I just wanted my mom.

I had surrendered.

The deceitful riptide of the fear of surrender lies to us. It creates an environment of trifling fear within our minds. It convinces us that asking for help will lead to a relinquishing of personal power while forcing us to give in to the will of others. ***All the lies we tell ourselves about lack of control keep us from the hidden truth: Surrender is a blessing.***

What if instead of exerting control, we just let go? What if we accepted the very thing our egos tell us to fear? What if we embraced surrender?

### Embracing Surrender

None of the things I feared transpired. In fact, asking for help led me to a more profound and emotionally intimate relationship with my parents. In my arrogance I had assumed I knew how my story would end—as though I could predict the future. There would be fussing, petty power struggles, and general aggravation for an entire week, and my relationship with my parents, so carefully crafted over the past few years, would change . . . for the worse. At the time I didn't realize that my concerns were trifles—unsubstantial and mostly imagined.

I did indeed heal under my parents' care and I internalized profound lessons about humility and dependency. My parents found new purpose in life, if only for a week, and once again experienced the satisfaction of caring for one of their own. It may be no surprise to anyone else that the bond we had always felt, parent to child, actually deepened. What astonished me even more was that the connection we had as adults changed for the better.

During that week of convalescence, Bill, Elaine, and Nora all had a chance to see each other at their best and their worst. My beloved independence hadn't disappeared at all; it was there in a much healthier form. My parents did indeed respect me. And had I not asked for their help, I would never have experienced my mother slipping her hand into mine as we walked bravely into the hospital that gray morning, nor would I have laughed with my father as he threatened to draw smiley faces on my bandages.

These memories will last a lifetime, and I would not trade them now for all the control in the world.

In his best-selling book *The Power of Now*, Eckhart Tolle writes that "surrender is the profound wisdom of *yielding* to rather than *opposing* the flow of life." (The italics are Tolle's.) Surrender is not about giving up or giving in. Tolle adds, "It is to relinquish inner resistance to what is."

Surrender doesn't have to be just about failure and loss. Those defeatist images have nothing to do with asking for help, a positive and loving act of self-respect and self-worth. Instead, think of surrender as a letting-go of your preconceptions about how things should be. Surrendering opens us to unseen possibilities that cannot possibly exist while we struggle against what is. My relationship with my parents probably would have remained the same as long as I continued to resist the truth of what was: Namely, that I had a need, and I could not control how it would be satisfied.

## TRY THIS    THE RIPTIDE OF SURRENDER

How has the riptide of fear or surrender shown up in your life? Ask yourself the following questions.

♦ Think of a time when you were worried that you might lose some of your independence if you asked for help. What were the circumstances then? Did you ask anyway?

♦ Describe a situation where you would have paid any price or met any requirement in order to receive help. What did you need? What kind of help did you receive? What was the cost to you?

♦ When have you been glad to surrender to the care of another person? What did you learn from that experience?

The flip side of this, of course, is that you could continue to seek control. John O'Donohue, author of *Anam Cara, A Book of Celtic Wisdom*, writes, "It is startling that we desperately hold on to what makes us miserable . . . We do not want to be cured, for that would mean moving into the unknown."

Surprise parties, sneezes, orgasms, a great night's sleep, laughter, and relaxing body massages are all gifts that only come when we let go and surrender. These simple and welcome blessings only hint at what's possible when we pull ourselves from the undertow caused by the fear of surrender.

## The Second Riptide: The Fear of Separation

James's hands were shaking. Head down, he seemed very different from the man I had coached two weeks earlier.

Then we had celebrated his new job with a marketing firm. All the fears James had held about selling his small business and going back to work for someone else seemed to have faded away as soon as he was hired. James was sure that with this new job he'd be able to pay his debts, including child support for his daughter, Marie.

Unfortunately the buyer of his business had subsequently decided against purchasing two major pieces of equipment, machines on which James was still making payments. They would have to be sold immediately. James figured that one day off each week for three consecutive weeks would give him enough time to sell the equipment. If not, James was at serious risk of missing loan payments. He was not at all sure he wanted to ask his new boss for such a big favor. What if he was fired from this new job? He was terrified by the fear of separation.

What is the lie spewed by this riptide? Like always, the deceptive current entices us with what we believe is truth: Not only are we born alone, we die alone. This seems to make sense to us, so we move deeper into the current as we continue to listen. Then the riptide snags us with the lie: If we are alone at the start and the end, then we must be alone in the in-between time, too.

We all want to be seen as part of something larger than ourselves, as a member of a team, a tribe, a society, a couple, a family. Within the group, we receive affirmation of our talents, skills, and gifts. We see our own value reflected in those around us. If we are cast out, we feel the abandonment profoundly. Indeed, banishment, or separation from the tribe, is so terrifying to us as humans that it has been, throughout history, a common alternative punishment to execution for capital crimes. Without the group, we have no one but ourselves.

In our ego-minds, the fear of separation convinces us that we are alone . . . very much alone. Any kind of division from those we've gathered around us, including family, friends, co-workers, and even complete strangers, seems to confirm this awful "truth."

Ask people why they don't ask for help, and the first answer is usually, "What if they say no? I might be rejected!" This fear of rejection is one manifestation of the fear of separation. As we consider asking for aid, each of us knows that our request may be refused or that we may be dismissed outright—an obvious rejection, to be sure. The ego translates this as not only a refusal of our need but a denunciation of ourselves and a denial that we are worthy of help. Of course, the rejection might have nothing to do with us at all, but the ego isn't likely to believe that. In our need and worry, we interpret rejection to mean, "You are on your own." In our fear, we silently add, ". . . once again."

James feared basic rejection, but he also had other concerns. In our session, he recounted the messages that his fear of separation was sending him: "You're alone in this, buddy.

You are going to get yourself fired. You're not going to be able to pay your debts. You won't be able to see your daughter again. No one is going to want to help you."

Poor guy—no wonder his hands were shaking! He was catastrophizing the situation, listening only to his fear, imagining the worst-case scenario. His initial terror at facing this problem alone (fear of separation) led to a greater desire to control the situation (fear of surrender).

### You Are Not Alone

**The hidden truth that this deceptive riptide, the fear of separation, doesn't want you to know is that you are not alone.** James was not alone, and neither are the rest of us.

Those who possess a spiritual outlook speak of the connectedness of all things. Many of the major religions contain a central belief in the constant presence of a supreme being who watches over all his/her creations. Others believe that we are all linked, one in the same, a small part in an all-encompassing system of energy. Still others embrace the comforting images of guardian angels and fairy godmothers who come to our aid, often to save us from ourselves. These are not just reassuring images for children at bedtime; they are archetypes that remind us, as adults, that we will always be cared for.

**TRY THIS**   DISPROVING THE FEAR OF SEPARATION

Try these suggestions for defeating the fear of separation and to confirm that you are not alone.

♦ If you believe in the here and now, formulate a hypothesis such as: "I am not alone." Then test it: Ask, and ask until you have enough evidence to support or deny your hypothesis.

♦ Search the Internet. We can find proof that we are not alone simply by conducting an online search for others who share our troubles.

♦ Call a meeting. Lay out your problem or concern in front of a group of trusted colleagues or friends. Most will come to your aid in some way if you only ask.

♦ Review your history. Create a major-events inventory, listing key accomplishments in your life: making the team, graduation, getting a job. Next to each, list the names of those people who helped you succeed.

♦ Watch for synchronicity in your life: Synchronicity is a coming-together of seemingly disparate events in a way that appears planned. I once suggested that a client might want to keep a journal to capture his thoughts during a time of great frustration. He rejected the idea, but that same night, he went for a walk in an unfamiliar part of town. Turning down a street lined with shops, he noticed that a small bookstore was the only shop open. The display at the entrance was a collection of blank journals! He ended up purchasing a journal, almost ready to believe that someone or something was looking out for him.

The notion that there are angels and fairy godmothers, let alone actual deities who care one iota for the troubles of humankind, may be hard for some to stomach. For those people, evidence is required to prove that they are not alone.

Sadly, for those bound by fear, the presence of God or human friendship often seems very far away. In these times it may be best to take a deep breath and that well-worn, frightening leap of faith. We will take time to explore that courageous act in a later chapter.

Those who refuse their fears and ask for assistance are relieved and often surprised to find that others are willing to help. This is, in fact, what happened in James's situation.

In preparing for the conversation with his boss, James made deliberate choices about the kind of language he wanted to use, as well as the mood he wanted to carry with him into the meeting. He was determined to come across as confident, respectful, and optimistic.

He began his conversation with his boss this way:

"I need your help. An unexpected situation has come up, and I thought that you and I could brainstorm some ways in which I might be able to deal with the problem. Would you be willing to help me out here?"

Notice that James didn't come in assuming he knew the answer that would solve his problem. He didn't ask for time off right away. Instead he chose to remain unattached to the outcome. That way he was able to stay open to new ways to solve his dilemma.

To James's great relief, his boss was very interested in helping him. Immediately James felt less alone.

He then went on to explain the problem. After a pause, James added that he could only come up with one option, which was to request some time off, but he thought that together they might be able to come up with a better alternative. After running through various scenarios, the two men decided that time off was the best, though perhaps not the most desirable, option in the situation.

It would be great to be able to say that James's boss was overjoyed to give him the time off, but it didn't happen that way. In fact, he was very unhappy with the situation, but he thought that James had handled it professionally and honestly. James had understood his boss's difficulties. As is often the case in work settings, an exchange was agreed upon. James received the time off, but only after committing to work on Saturdays to compensate.

James walked away from the conversation with a reaffirmation that he was no longer alone, that he had made the right choice in accepting this job. He deeply appreciated the sacrifice his boss was making for him, and he gained renewed confidence in his own value to the company. Interestingly, the agreement reinforced his membership within the team, since he soon discovered that many of his co-workers could also be found working in the office on Saturdays.

A precedent was set in James's relationship with his boss. Boss and employee began to understand that they could work through most issues together, which served as the beginning of a business relationship that changed over time to one based in friendship and trust. James might never have discovered this had he not asked for the help he needed.

Asking for help is often the very last thing we want to do, yet it is just as often the very first step we should take. Denying our need because of the lies spread by the fear of separation only keeps us farther away from the circle of friendship and community.

## TRY THIS    THE FEAR OF SEPARATION

The second riptide, the fear of separation, affects us all. At some level, we fear being alone. Answer the following questions to get an idea how this riptide manifests in your life.

◆ With whom are you most comfortable asking for help? What is it about your relationship that makes it easier for you to ask?

◆ What relationship(s) would you hate to lose most? Would your relationship(s) withstand a mayday cry from you? Why or why not?

◆ Think of a time when you needed help and help came your way. How did that situation prove to you that you were not alone?

## The Third Riptide: The Fear of Shame

By now the dreadful riptides of surrender and separation probably sound familiar to you. You may even be able to feel the residue of their deceptions in your life as you recall the times you attempted to make your own requests. There is one more riptide to explore: the fear of shame.

Public shame is a penalty most of us are unwilling to tolerate. We've come a long way from locking scofflaws in the village stocks, but the threat of public humiliation is still with us. It rises up when our dark sides are on view for all to see.

Sometimes referred to as the fear of the shadow or of the dark side, this fear is based on more of Carl Jung's work. He described the shadow as being that part of ourselves we strive to keep hidden. In our shame, he explains, we hide the dark parts of ourselves that have been rejected for lack of love. Jung's central point was that "the shadow is the person you would rather not be."

The fear of shame convinces us that we are not worthy. It co-opts the truth that we are flawed and then persuades us that the flaw must forever remain hidden. If the "truth" gets out, you will, without a doubt, be mortified and publicly shamed. Indeed, we work hard to hide our shadows, those habits, behaviors, viewpoints, and idiosyncrasies that we've decided would seem reprehensible to others. We expend tremendous energy denying what is, hiding it even from ourselves. The last thing we want to do is to reveal our weaknesses to others by asking for help. For some, this is tantamount to professional or social suicide!

The fear of shame can also lead to a different kind of self-sabotage, the deadly kind. In South Africa, where AIDS has infected 20% of its adult population, the shame is too much to bear. In an article written for the November 26, 2006 *Chicago Tribune*, Laurie Goering writes about the epidemic, "the disease remains such a mark of shame that many people prefer to die rather than seek treatment." Such is the power of this fear. Even when faced with death, *metus gravis,* some would prefer to pretend that help is not required.

Debbie Ford, author of *The Dark Side of the Light Chasers,* writes that the shadow "contains those dark aspects that we believe are not acceptable to our family, friends, and most importantly, ourselves . . . The message we get from this is simple: there is something wrong with me." That can be a very good thing.

As Jung did before her, Ford believes these dark aspects

are opportunities to grow and learn. Instead of being ignored or repressed, they should be acknowledged, examined, accepted, and, most important, owned. By owning these shameful secrets we set ourselves free and enable new possibilities to enter our lives—especially the possibility of asking for help.

## The Shame of Neediness

Each of us is ashamed of different aspects of our lives. Being seen as needy, in particular, is something that we avoid at all costs. When we reveal neediness, the dirty, dark corners of our psyche come into high relief. Dripping with neediness, our mayday signals are easily noticed—and as easily rejected—by potential helpmates. In an effort to disguise our neediness, we might become demanding, like I did when I told my boyfriend that I needed him to stay with me during my convalescence. More so than men, women fear being seen as needy. Being needy is viewed as the kiss of death to most romantic relationships, and single women work doubly hard to steer clear of the label.

Melanie is needy. Everyone sees it but her. An hour before her best friend's wedding, she asked Olivia, the bride-to-be, to stop getting dressed and help her instead. Years later, when Olivia was waiting for news about her beloved husband's cancer diagnosis, Melanie called the house over and over again, in effect keeping the phone line tied up. And when she learned that Olivia's husband had passed away, Melanie monopolized her time during the funeral visitation. Her focus ostensibly was on Olivia, but Melanie's inappropriate requests for help and support proved that it was really all about her.

With behavior like this, Melanie was labeled high maintenance by her friends and by the men she chose to date. Overly dependent, controlling, and desperate, Melanie had a hard time keeping any kind of romantic relationship alive. Melanie would have been embarrassed to know that others saw her as just too much trouble. Possessiveness, demanding, clinginess, and self-involvement all are qualities of needy people and Melanie had these in abundance.

"Neediness is created when perfectly sane and normal people do not get their needs met." So writes John Gray, author of *Men Are from Mars, Women Are from Venus*. There is no getting around it. If you are human, you have needs, and you have the potential to become needy. Gray suggests that one reason we become controlling is because we have not properly expressed what it is we need. We have not asked for what we need.

At some point in our lives, we experience a gap between our current existence and what could be—a need. Over time, needs that go unexpressed and unanswered can mutate into unflattering and unattractive neediness.

## Gillian's Story

Gillian had created a wonderful life for herself. A graduate of a prestigious university, she was now the proud proprietor of a small yet very successful business in the heart of London, England. She had married her high school sweetheart and was the mother of two rambunctious young boys.

Gillian seemed to have the perfect life . . . on the surface. Sadly, her husband, a charming and brilliant man, was plagued by a recurring illness that forced Gillian to take the lead in many family decisions. During one particularly difficult period, Gillian's husband was hospitalized for treatment, leaving her to run the house, handle the kids, pay the bills, manage the business alone, and worry about and care for her husband. If ever there was a person who needed help, it was Gillian. It wasn't until she found herself weeping uncontrollably at a neighbor's house one night that she finally admitted she needed help.

We all go through periods like this, but what interested me about Gillian's story was that her neighbor, Cheryl, a woman she'd known for years, came right out and asked why she had never called for help.

Gillian's response was typical and very stiff-upper-lip British: "I was so ashamed. I should have been able to handle it."

In response, Cheryl simply took Gillian's hand and told her, "Don't worry, I am going to help you."

Their friendship, which began based on the proximity of their houses, blossomed through the new closeness in their hearts. Cheryl had always been there for Gillian, she just never knew help was needed. You might be surprised by how much help is yours for the asking. What you receive in return is of more value than the fragile ego you protect by remaining quiet.

### You Are Worthy

Gillian's shadow was not so terrible, of course, though she thought it was. ***No matter who we are, we are worthy of the help we seek. This is the hidden truth that the fear of shame keeps from us.***

Many years ago I coached a woman who believed she was not deserving of help. Nearing retirement, Jenna still had many people who relied on her, yet she refused to depend on anyone else. I thought, perhaps, that she, a devout Christian, would seek help from God. I asked her how she prayed. She told me that she always prayed for others but never for herself. "I'm not starving, I am not living on the street. God has others He should be caring for instead of me."

Who are we to decide whom God should help? Who are

we to decide that our problems are undeserving of help? Worthiness is not based on how difficult life is. Worthiness is not a test used to determine whether or not you should be cared for. Your needs warrant resolution. You deserve to ask for the help you need.

**TRY THIS**    **THE FEAR OF SHAME**

Your answers to the following questions will help you understand your own fears of shame.

◆ Make a list of those behaviors, habits, or unflattering qualities that you keep hidden from others.

◆ How has the fear of shame interfered with your relationships in the past? How has it limited your relationships at home or at work?

◆ If someone agrees to your request for help, what is the worst-case scenario if they happen to observe your shadow? What is the best-case scenario?

The Riptide Matrix summarizes the fears that keep us from connecting, from learning and growing, from asking for the help we deserve.

# THE RIPTIDE MATRIX

| | The Riptide of Surrender | The Riptide of Separation | The Riptide of Shame |
|---|---|---|---|
| The Lie | All control is good and the loss of control is very bad. | You have always been alone and you are alone now. | You are flawed. You must never let anyone see your flaws or they will be repulsed by you. |
| Related Concerns | Loss of independence<br><br>Concern over the price tag for help<br><br>Fear of the unknown<br><br>Loss of control over how things are done<br><br>Loss of financial security | Risk of losing one's job<br><br>Banishment from the family or community<br><br>Fear of rejection | Concern over revealing one's weaknesses<br><br>Feeling unworthy or undeserving |
| The Truth Behind the Fear | Control is impossible and surrender can be glorious. | You are not alone. | You are worthy of help. |

Lost in fear and weak with need, we lose sight of the shore. Smothered by the riptides, we swallow the lies told by fear. The three riptides desperately want to convince you that loss of control is a bad thing, that you will be separated from those you love, and that you will experience excruciating shame—all because you asked for help. Yet these are trivial, trifling fears, out of proportion to the facts of the situation. Yet we allow ourselves to be swallowed up by the fear, tossed and turned in the wake of a deceptive riptide.

It doesn't have to be that way. You have the choice to see the truth: Surrender is a blessing, you are not alone, and you are worthy of your requests.

# CHAPTER 3

# WHY WE SHOULD ASK

■ ■ ■ — — ■ ■ ■

A friend is someone who will help you move.
A real friend is someone who will help you move a body.
*Unknown*

No wonder we don't ask for help! We lack instruction, models, awareness, and even permission to ask. Our fears conspire to distract and confuse us, sometimes keeping us from fulfilling even basic needs. These same obstructions also keep us blind to forgotten rewards, benefits, and blessings that come when we ignore the fear and embrace help. The moment we decide to make a mayday call, we set into motion a creative energy that brings us into the realm of possibilities. Something new is brought into reality.

Sending out a mayday call, often the last step you want to take, is just as often the very first one you should consider. Nowhere is it written that you have to solve all of your problems by yourself. Do not buy into the lies told by the riptide fears of surrender, separation, and shame. The truth is that you are truly worthy of your requests for aid. You are cared for, you are not alone, and you are blessed. These are wonderful gifts in and of themselves. When we ask for help, even more wonderful things can happen. What follows are seven priceless gifts of love, flow, and simplicity that can be yours—if you only ask.

## Asking for Help = Help

The dishes get done, the report gets proofed, the client gets picked up at the airport, and you get to bed at a decent hour. Imagine what your days would be like if you got the help you needed! Your daily to-do list would not appear so daunting and you might actually fit it all in and still have time to spare.

A Biblical passage reads, "Ask and you shall receive. Seek and you shall find. Knock and the door will be opened to you. For every one that asks will receive; and he that seeks shall find; and to him that knocks it shall be opened" (Matthew 7:7–8). I'm no theologian, but I'm pretty certain Christ wasn't advising us to keep quiet and deny our needs. He was trying to teach us to *actively reach* for all that is possible. The essential requirement here is to be involved. Before help arrives, we have to actively ask, seek, or knock.

Lives can be saved if we do our part and send out the mayday signal. Consider the submariners aboard the *Kursk*, the Russian submarine that foundered in August of 2000. During the days that followed her very real mayday cry, the world was forced to wait in anguish while the Russian Navy refused to ask for the help it needed to save the men aboard. A few days after the disaster, there was one particular heart-wrenching moment when Emma Yevdokimova demanded of President Putin: "Why didn't they ask for foreign help?" Emma is the mother of Oleg, one of the 118 submariners who died. Most salvage experts agree that the deaths of many of these men could have been avoided had the Russian Navy simply asked.

Thankfully, most of our needs are not so dire. Mostly, we need help with changing the oil, shoveling the walk, balancing accounts, even caring for the ill. Everything is possible, but only if we ask can it become probable.

## Asking for Help = More Energy, Less Exhaustion

Most of us are tired. There never seems to be enough time to accomplish everything on the to-do list. The demands of family, friends, and work never seem to go away and they often conflict. For many of us, it's a tangled mess. This isn't anything new to you, I'm sure. Asking for a hand is one way to untangle the knots and give ourselves a chance to rest and recover.

Years ago I received an interesting call from a potential client. Barely able to hear him on the phone—his voice was so weak—I soon learned that John was dangerously ill. A senior vice president in a large multinational technology firm, John was calling from a hotel in New York, even though he was really based in California. He confessed that he was suffering with his third bout of pneumonia in seven months. Justifiably worried, his boss in London had insisted that John head to the nearest hospital. Instead, John asked the hotel staff to call a doctor, whose remedy was "either stay in bed in this hotel for the next four weeks, or I will have you taken to the hospital for recovery." John had chosen the hotel room.

His life was a mess. Living alone, thousands of miles away from his normal support system of family and friends, John forced himself to do too much. Work was relentless and his travel in so many time zones didn't help matters. John was physically exhausted, so much so that his body was unable to fend off hazardous viruses for months on end.

As a coach in high-pressure business environments, I see this tale play out all too often. There's plenty of help to be had. But people don't see it because they've fallen for the lies told by their fears of surrender, shame, and separation.

Many convince themselves that they just need to work longer hours or be better organized. "Insanity is the logic of an accurate mind overtaxed," said Oliver Wendell Holmes. No kidding! When we are overstressed, logic eludes us. Our decisions become mistakes. Our judgment is suspect. Doing more and doing it longer aren't the answer. Requesting help is often the only way to avoid exhaustion and retain our health.

We don't do ourselves any favors when we insist on doing it all ourselves. We can limit the opportunities for others to contribute. Our energy gets spent unwisely and we exhaust ourselves by simply doing too much. Taking the longer view, asking for help, allowing others to give of themselves, can save us time and energy.

Asking for help is, as you can imagine, what John and I spent much of our time discussing. Shortly after regaining his health, John was able to restructure his life and begin again—with the help of his employer and co-workers.

## Asking for Help = Flow

When it comes to sending out a mayday cry, sometimes we too have to sit back, relax, and let go. When we do, we return to the flow of life. It is our overrated desire for control that keeps us from living life as it was meant to be.

Mihaly Csikszentmihalyi, a psychology professor from the University of Chicago and author of *Flow: The Psychology of Optimal Experience* has defined flow as "being completely involved in an activity for its own sake. The ego falls away. Time flies. Every action, movement, and thought follows inevitably from the previous one, like playing jazz. Your whole being is involved, and you're using your skills to the utmost."

Athletes recognize this experience of flow as "being in the zone." Musicians refer to it as "being in the groove." Those with a strong spiritual perspective interpret flow as a time when they act from spirit rather than ego. Whatever we call it, being in the flow is an undeniable experience of effortlessness and joy.

Being in the flow is actually easy. Being out of the flow is what's hard. Often our own denial and rejection of our imperfections pull us from flow, and it is at these times that the ego is fully involved—the exact opposite of Csikszentmihalyi's vision. Time does not fly. Actions, movements, or thoughts do not follow the previous ones. Life gets difficult and we get tired.

Not surprisingly, the metaphor of a river is often used to explain flow. In the flow of life, we float happily and safely with the water. However, when we need help, we find ourselves sitting on the riverbank watching the water rush by.

When I fought against asking my parents to care for me immediately after my surgery, I removed myself from the flow of life. For an entire week, I would be unable to do for myself. Life had presented me with an opportunity to grow, to learn, and to deepen my relationship with my parents. Ego-bound, I resisted this chance and chose instead to rely on someone else—which didn't quite work out. In trying to control the situation, I pulled myself from the river of life. I didn't return to it again until I finally let go in the middle of the night in a darkened hospital room.

Flow, being in the zone or the groove, requires us to ride along with, not fight, life. Trying too hard to control any situation or person immediately removes us from the flow. Resisting asking for help, believing that you can handle everything yourself, and striving for control are futile acts. Oftentimes, broadcasting a mayday call is what will return you to this place of effortlessness and joy.

## Asking for Help = Happiness for Others

Maria was a new vice president leading a team of experienced managers and staff. She admitted to me that she was intimidated by their know-how and familiarity with their customers. Maria thought she would have to pull them into line, or they would take advantage of her inexperience. She asked, "Isn't it my job to lead them and tell them what to do?" In reply, I asked, "Wouldn't you rather capitalize on what they know?" I suggested that she might acknowledge the truth of her inexperience instead of resisting it, and then ask for her team's help. "Ask them to talk about their secret skills, special areas of expertise that they could bring to the project."

Maria did just that. Six weeks later, Tyree, her most senior manager, came to her saying, "This is the best project I've been on in a long while. We all feel as though we are helping make this work."

Tyree and his co-workers were thrilled to add to the success of the project. They felt as though their individual, unique gifts were being used to their utmost. They got to practice skills that had been hidden from others and they were able to show what they could do—beyond their traditional roles.

We all have exceptional gifts, talents, and abilities. Being asked to contribute gives us a chance to display these capabilities. It becomes an opportunity for us to demonstrate our inner strengths, and even perhaps, to fulfill our life purpose.

Any time you send out a mayday signal, you actually offer a gift to your helpmate: a chance to be happy.

## Practicing Asking For Help = Proficiency

Baseball players spend a lot of time practicing in the batting cage. Dancers spend hours each week rehearsing. Parents-to-be practice breathing techniques over and over again. Practice doesn't always make perfect, but it sure does make some things easier.

Our comfort in any task or skill increases as we become more proficient. The same holds for requests for help. With enough effort, we might even get good at it.

The acquisition of a new skill is rarely easy, and as you learn how to ask for help, expect to experience frustration and impatience with yourself. Initial efforts may be clumsy or awkward. If you persevere, remaining deliberate in your requests for help, you can achieve a level of comfort. You might even become so proficient that you can teach the skill to others.

## Asking for Help = Personal Growth

Ebeneezer Scrooge, the infamous curmudgeon of Charles Dickens' imagination, learned the hard way how wonderful it is to give generously. In the course of 100 pages, his character is forced to mature and grow. His spiritual challenges opened his heart and his wallet. By the end of the book, he is a changed man. For most of us, learning to be generous is not nearly as hard as learning how to ask for help when we need it.

By its very nature, asking for that leg up is a test that is more deeply personal. It requires that we face fears that elicit our most profound memories of being lost or rejected, being controlled, and being humiliated. The challenge is to make a deliberate choice to move beyond these haunting memories.

Kieran was a bear of a boss. Possessing a wicked wit, he enjoyed the intellectual challenge of argument a bit too much. His favorite strategy was to intimidate his opponents with his clever humor and brilliant use of logic. I knew none of this when I first met him at a social event. As a point of conversation, I suggested that he consider hiring a coach. He did decide to hire me—albeit eighteen months later. Seriously unhappy, he asked me to help him.

I agreed, and suggested that he involve his team, too. Kieran resisted, concerned that the response might not be positive. After a few months, he relented and decided it was time to ask for their help. He went to each person and asked for feedback on his performance as a leader. This was humbling for Kieran. It brought up fears of surrender and shame. Inside, he knew he wasn't the best leader for these men and women.

The feedback from his co-workers was brutal but—just like Scrooge's ghosts—they elicited change. He soon realized that his love of argument separated him from the very people who were supposed to help him succeed: his team. Kieran made a dramatic turnaround simply by becoming an advocate of help, for himself and his direct reports. As painful as this was for him, he did grow—and all because he finally asked for help.

We spontaneously evolve when we send out a mayday call. The change starts the moment we decide to ask—well before we actually use words to express our need.

## Asking for Help = Transformed Relationships

Perhaps the most overlooked benefit that comes from asking for help is that it transforms our relationships. Kieran's relationships with his co-workers shifted substantially because he asked. Remember James? As soon as he requested time off, his relationship with his boss shifted—for the better. And Gillian? Her acquaintance with a neighbor quickly grew into a priceless friendship.

What is it about asking for help that transforms the superficial to the profound? Two ingredients are required to create this alchemy within our relationships: vulnerability and empathy.

Anytime we ask for help, we display a degree of openness that is both revealing and inviting. In effect, we say to our potential helpmate, "I confess to you that I need something from you. I admit to us both that I cannot do this alone." We acknowledge our humanity: imperfections and all. A deliberate willingness to remain open and vulnerable silences our egos. Vulnerability reigns in our pride and makes room in our hearts for a new level of connection or intimacy.

Friendships begin, existing ones can deepen, and romances can blossom when each party opens up and reveals themselves. That's exactly what happened in James's and Gillian's stories. Both confessed an inability to fulfill a need and in doing so they unconsciously invited in the energy and creativity of their helpmates.

Vulnerability engenders empathy in the hearts of our helpers. According to *Webster's New World Dictionary*, empathy is "an ability to share in another's emotions, thoughts or feelings." With empathy, we virtually experience another person's anguish. It propels us to listen closely, to feel for his or her predicament. Together, the combination of your vulnerability and your helpmate's empathy create a space for new conversations and, ultimately, a new future.

Some of the transformations that take place in our relationships are disappointing and even difficult. I've already admitted that I lost one romance over the help I needed. As hard as that was, it was exactly what needed to happen. The relationship had gone on too long and had stopped growing. It was time to end it and my request served as the catalyst. The experience became a lesson not just for me, but for my friend as well. Years later, we reconnected and had a chance to talk through what had happened. Apologies all around. Now our friendship is even stronger than before. Even if we had not reconnected, I do not regret what happened.

Like me, your own requests for help might reveal what

you've worked hard to keep hidden in your relationships. You may come to realize that the people in your life are the wrong ones. You may recognize that the friends and family you'd like to count on have needs greater than your own. You may see that help comes from surprising sources and that perhaps, just perhaps, these new sources could become new friends.

Sending out a mayday request has the potential to create of life of flow, simplicity, and rest. With practice, it can become easier. Our mayday cries reveal what we have kept hidden and, in the process, create a new future for our relationships with all those we come in contact with.

### TRY THIS    THE BENEFITS YOU'VE EXPERIENCED

Most people have asked for help in the past at some point in their lives. How has asking for help changed your life—for the better?

◆ How has asking for help allowed you to fulfill a need or achieve a goal?

◆ How has asking for help allowed you to find balance or a bit more energy?

◆ How has asking for help returned you to the flow? How has it enabled you to find your groove again?

◆ How has asking for help made other people happy?

◆ How has asking for help stretched you and shown you what you are capable of?

◆ How has asking for help transformed your relationships? How has it changed your personal relationships? How has it affected your professional relationships?

# CHAPTER 4

# ANCHORING YOURSELF

■ ■ ■ ━ ━ ━ ■ ■ ■

Great necessities call out great virtues.
*Abigail Adams*

Amy loved her father dearly. Aron had always been her greatest supporter, cheering her on when she ran for class president and comforting her after her divorce. He had been both mother and father to her ever since Amy's mother passed away decades before. And now, Amy had the chance to repay him (as if that's even possible) for all his kindness, generosity, and love. Aron had Alzheimer's disease and Amy was his caregiver.

At first it had been painful to watch the man she most admired disappear into the illness. She secretly wept when she had to remind him what spackle was and how to use it. "He had practically built the family house with his own two hands and now he couldn't remember spackle." She cried. There were also frustrating times when Aron forgot to meet her as planned or became lost along the way. Most difficult of all was watching her father shrink before her eyes. The disease had made him small and frail.

A day nurse was hired to care for him while she was at work, and at night, Amy would return home to fix and feed him dinner. Afterward, she would help him to his chair. Once he was comfortable, she'd put on some music. If Aron was in a quiet mood, she might be able to do a little reading. But if he was talkative, she would listen to him as he relived a memory from his past. Sometimes, he would ask Amy where her mother was. The first few times he did this, she would gently remind him that his wife had passed many years before. It would upset him to hear, all over again, that she was gone. Eventually, Amy learned to just say that her mother had gone out to do some shopping. Aron would be satisfied with this and within a few moments would have forgotten all about his question.

At 56, Amy was exhausted and sad. She would have her father only for a little while longer. At the same time, she knew the man he had been was long gone. She confessed, "He doesn't even know who he is anymore, and I don't know either. He's certainly not the dad I've always known and counted on." Asked how she was doing, she said, "I need help. I can't take care of him by myself anymore and I'm not quite ready to move him into assisted living. I just need a break now and then, but I feel too guilty leaving him with someone else."

"Where is the guilt coming from?" I asked. Amy replied, "Because I should be the one to take care of him. I'm all he has left. How can I go and enjoy myself knowing he's sitting at home lost in his memories?"

Amy's guilt prevented her from caring for herself. As much as she loved her father, she felt a heavy obligation to look after him. Her father may have lost his mental capacities, but Amy had lost a sense of proportion and balance. Everyone needs a respite from life's responsibilities now and then. Her father wasn't stopping her from getting help and going out; her own emotions were doing that.

## Getting Motivated to Ask

In order for Amy, or any of us for that matter, to ask for help, we need to be motivated to do so. Nothing motivates us more than our emotions. In fact, the root of the words *motivate* and *emotion* are the same. Emotion is all about motion, movement, action, and behavior. Emotions are catalysts that direct us to act, to react, and to behave.

Our review of the three riptides of surrender, separation, and shame was intended to shine a light on the negative and fearful emotions that stop us from asking for help. These fear-based emotions slam on the brakes and prevent us from getting what we need. In order to ask for help, different emotional states are required. These new emotions don't inhibit, instead they motivate us to ask for what we need.

## The Anchoring Principles

For the most part, emotions are reactive in nature. We see something or experience some kind of event or stimulus, and we react with an interpretation and a feeling. In turn, we are compelled to take some kind of action. For example, if I see a spider, I react with a thought that spiders are creepy and the emotion of fear. My eyes widen, my breathing shortens, the little hairs on the back of my neck stand up, and I become very pale. I feel a strong motivation to run like crazy. I may even scream. My fear has affected me physically.

*The first anchoring principle is that emotions affect body and language.* You may recognize this as the classic mind/body connection, or more accurately, *emotion/body/language connection.* The Newfield Network, a transformational learning company for leaders located in Boulder, Colorado, has explored the emotion/body/language connection extensively. Newfield uses this principle as they work with, train, and coach leaders from all over the world. When our emotions are engaged, they affect us directly. Actions we take will reflect, even betray, what we feel inside. Any of the words we unconsciously choose will reflect the emotions we feel. Hence my scream—not exactly a word, but close enough—and my inclination to run from spiders.

Typically, emotions also affect our body and language in *specific* ways. Certain actions and behaviors are associated with many emotional states. Fear has its own reactive behaviors: the well-known fight-or-flight response. When we experience fear, we either run, avoiding the problem entirely, or we fight, facing it head on. This reaction applies to both *metus gravis* and *levis,* grave and trifling fear.

Understanding that emotions affect us physically and alter the words we use, fear is the last place we want to go when we need to ask for assistance. Fear does not compel us to ask; if anything, it usually stops us from requesting what we need. If we do squeeze out a mayday cry, the words that fall from our lips will be dripping with it. Our voices will sound frightened, apprehensive, or even defensive. The words we choose will be wrong, fearful, and inarticulate. As long as fear is present, our bodies will reflexively display it. Fear may cause us to cast our eyes downward instead of straight ahead. Fear may move us to fold our arms or fidget with our hands. Unless we are truly expert in hiding our emotions—and most of us are not—our helpmates may easily perceive our weakened state of worry and anxiety.

In Amy's case, the emotion of guilt affected her deeply. Typically, guilt, a combined feeling of shame and responsibility, moves us to either ask for forgiveness or punishment. When there is no one to forgive us—in Amy's case, her father was unable to offer her absolution—our reactive behavior is to punish ourselves. Amy felt ashamed and guilty for being frustrated and impatient. She believed she deserved punishment, so she locked herself away in the self-imposed prison that was her father's house. Physically, the feeling of guilt moved her to speak differently. Her voice changed, becoming more strident and strained. Her eyes appeared lifeless, without energy or sparkle. Self-reproach roughened her actions, making them brusquely efficient.

Before Amy could ask for help, she needed to generate a new, more powerful, emotional state, one rooted in love for herself and her father.

Thankfully, emotions are not just reactive in nature, they can also be deliberate: We can intentionally choose to feel differently. For example, the moment I notice that I feel frustration about a mess that my dog has made, I have a choice to make. I can continue to carry the knee-jerk frustration and its corresponding behaviors (grumbling, stomping around the house), or I can choose a different emotional state. I could deliberately decide to be curious as to whether she was feeling all right. Or, I might choose to be indifferent, simply cleaning the mess without comment. Regardless of my choice, I am no longer at the mercy of the reactive quality of emotion. Instead, I can intentionally select an emotional state that serves me better. In this same way, we can choose to remain afraid to ask for what we need, or we can proactively choose different emotional states. ***This is the second of the anchoring principles of the Mayday! process: Get the emotion right and the right words and deeds will follow.***

Making deliberate emotional shifts is not always easy. The typical approach is to talk ourselves out of one emotional state and into another. Sometimes this works, but often it doesn't. It's like saying we can talk ourselves out of being in love with someone, a highly unlikely approach. Instead, intentional emotional shifts often require an action, a physical movement or gesture that alters our emotional states. That's why, after a heartbreak, we rip up photos or put away sentimental gifts from our ex. We feel an instinctive need to *do* something, anything to move on, to feel differently.

*Fear won't motivate us to ask for what we need. So it becomes necessary for us to deliberately, with intention, choose different emotional states, the kind that will move us to ask for what we need.*

**TRY THIS   INTENTIONAL EMOTIONS**

The ability to shift from one emotional state to another is a learned behavior. Spend a moment examining your own experiences.

♦ Think of a time when you controlled your emotional response to a situation. What happened?

♦ How did you decide the first emotion was not appropriate?

♦ How did you go about shifting from one emotional state to another? Was it purely an intellectual or mental shift? Or did you do something physically to make the change happen?

## Emotional Discomfort

At no time should you construe the anchoring principles to mean that you have permission to become cut off from your own feelings. Making a shift from one emotional state to another is not always recommended. Suppression (conscious rejection or exclusion) and repression (unconscious rejection or exclusion) of your emotions are rarely wise. Sometimes in your life it will be important to remain angry or reticent or frustrated. However, when it comes to asking for help, a shift from one emotional state to another is advisable.

The emotions and moods we experience are natural aspects of life, yet we have become uncomfortable talking about and expressing them, especially in the workplace. Often, they are noted only when they are expressed at a highly passionate level. Then we say someone is being "emotional." Some people respond with discomfort and prefer that emotions be removed from the office altogether. "Do your work, stay focused, and leave your feelings at home," they warn. That might seem efficient, but it's not possible. Emotions never leave us, no matter how hard we try to ignore them.

Confounding our discomfort is the fact that, as a culture, we have become emotionally illiterate. Instead of distinguishing between anger and indignation, we say we're "pissed off." Instead of specifying that we are frustrated or aggravated, we say, we're "in a bad mood." We even use the word *love* to describe everything from gluttony (I'd love a third donut) to romantic attachment (He is the love of my life).

Being able to accurately name an emotion and describe it is important, especially as we prepare to send out a mayday cry. When we confuse the meanings of different emotions, we reduce our understanding of what is possible. If we can distinguish one emotion from another, then we are better able to determine what is preventing us from getting the help we need.

As you read further, you will learn distinctions between *sympathy* and *compassion*, *hope* and *faith*, and *appreciation* and *gratitude*. We use these words interchangeably in general conversation. But when it comes to asking for help and applying the *Mayday!* process, we need to be more rigorous in their use.

It's easy to reacquaint yourself with your emotions. Spend time reading the Common Emotions list, below. Use it in meetings and see how many you can identify in the room. Use it at home and figure out whether your family is a happy one or perhaps even a curious one. Begin to see emotion as an integral and necessary part of your life. Each has the power to propel us, or limit us, as we create new futures.

### Common Emotions

♦ Are you happy, pleased, glad, joyful, contented, relaxed,

calm, blissful, exultant, delighted, cheery, jovial, optimistic, joyous, ecstatic, glad?

♦ Are you at peace, satisfied, serene, comfortable, peaceful, relaxed, passive, calm?

♦ Are you sad, depressed, low, dismal, moody, sulky, defeated, pessimistic, miserable, heartbroken, distressed?

♦ Are you hurt, offended, upset, disappointed, heartbroken, crushed, miffed, wounded?

♦ Are you angry, annoyed, irritated, cross, livid, frustrated, indignant, irate, furious, fuming, enraged, cross, furious, incensed, outraged?

♦ Are you afraid, fearful, frightened, timid, cautious, concerned, apprehensive, alarmed, nervous, anxious, worried, hesitant, threatened, scared, petrified, terrified?

♦ Are you loving, accepting, understanding, fond, devoted, caring, affectionate, adoring, doting, warm, tender, passionate?

♦ Are you interested, involved, concerned, attracted, enthusiastic, intrigued, absorbed, excited, inquisitive, intent, fascinated, engrossed?

♦ Are you confident, certain, positive, convinced, secure, independent, brave, courageous, strong, empowered, proud?

♦ Are you doubtful, uncertain, unsure, disbelieving, cynical, indecisive, wavering, insecure, skeptical, dubious, suspicious, distrustful?

♦ Do you feel shame, dishonored, uncomfortable, embarrassed, humiliated, weak?

## Seed Emotions

Though all emotions generate some kind of action or behavior, not all result in bold moves or profound change. Some only move us to minor actions. Emotions can be classified into one of three levels, with each level defined by how great the resulting action is.

*Passive emotions*, such as contentment and pleasure do not elicit much in the way of action from anyone. At the most, they might encourage us to lay back, kick up our feet, and smile. Our words will reflect our satisfaction, but there will be little power behind them.

*Functioning emotions* are a bit more . . . emotive. Eagerness, enthusiasm, and curiosity are examples of emotions with more substantial associated actions. Acting from these, we might cheer on a friend or two or we might step up and begin something new. But these emotions do not change the world.

As relatively ineffective as they are, passive and functioning emotions serve a critical function. They operate as seed emotions for their big brothers, the virtues.

*Virtues* are emotional engines designed to elevate us to the best we can be. These emotional powerhouses grab us and never let us go—at least not without a great deal of internal anguish. They are addictive to our bodies and our minds. They motivate us to audacious and courageous acts, and to speak with that same bravery. ***Virtuous emotional states are the ones that move us to ask for what we need and to do it with clarity, strength, and purpose.***

In particular, three seed emotions are critical for the success of our mayday calls. They are

♦ Sympathy, which leads to the virtue of compassion.

♦ Hope, which leads to the virtue of faith.

♦ Appreciation, which leads to the virtue of gratitude.

By themselves, each seed emotion is relatively ineffective. Sympathy, hope, and appreciation are admirable and loving emotions, but when it comes to overcoming the fears of surrender, separation, and shame, they are weaklings. To make our requests, to fulfill our needs through the assistance of another person, we require more powerful emotional states.

Seed emotions will not compel you to ask for help. Just as a flower seed needs water, each seed emotion needs to be cultivated with the help of another ingredient. Combine these emotional seeds with an action and they will grow into powerful virtues. When that happens, we are changed forever, life appears differently, and we automatically move to create the lives we've always wanted. When virtue is in place, asking for help loses its intimidation factor. Instead, crying mayday becomes an act of self-respect.

## Applied Virtue

Not a popular word nowadays, *virtue* conjures images of corsets and stiff collars. For some it may elicit memories with more formal religious connotations. *Virtue*, a seemingly old-fashioned concept, doesn't appear to belong in the twenty-first century; yet, virtue does and can exist, every day and in almost every challenge . . . especially in asking for help.

Most definitions of the word address moral excellence and commendable traits or qualities. Josef Pieper, a philosopher and survivor of Nazi Germany, wrote that virtues enable a person "to attain the furthest potentialities of his nature." "Furthest potentialities"—this phrase inspires me and reminds me that, even in difficult situations, we all can be great.

Virtue encompasses the highest qualities of humanity and leads us to our best selves. It gives us permission to live from our own personal wisdom. It guides us down a path of possibilities, even those that exist in our darkest moments, when our need is great and when help seems far away. Then virtue changes us forever.

Four properties give virtue its mysterious power. An understanding of these qualities (based on the works of Dr. Pieper and Gilbert Meilaender, another world-renowned ethicist) explains why virtue brings on miraculous change. The combination of these four properties takes virtue from the obsolete to the applicable. No longer the province of saints and prophets, these super emotional states can belong to us common folk, too. These applied virtues (AVs) can be used in even the most mundane situations. AVs are especially useful when we find we cannot do it alone and need to reach out for a helping hand.

***Applied virtue, like emotion, affects body and language.*** The greatness of their virtuous acts attracts us to people like the Dalai Lama and Mother Teresa. These very flawed people have shown us how to be our best selves through their intrepid and courageous acts. Their words are kind, open, and inviting. They have proved that personal greatness is possible through a life of integrity and love rather than one of fear. Though we may not have classic archetypes to show us how to ask for what we need, we do have a few virtuous role models that have shown us how to live.

Remember Amy? Her compassion for her father moved her to sacrifice a great deal. This was a purely virtuous act. That virtue still lives on, though it may be buried beneath the physical exhaustion she feels. What Amy didn't quite understand is that her ego and the fear of shame were hard at work, making her question the most generous of deeds.

***Applied virtue can be learned.*** Think of each applied virtue as a kind of life skill. Less specific in nature than, say, paying your taxes or reading a map, virtues can be applied according to the needs of each situation. For example, just as we are born not knowing how to sew on a button, we may not know how to be generous. Yet we can learn how to do both.

Often our lessons begin at a young age through examples delivered by our parents or teachers or through archetypal stories. But none of us really comprehends the power of an applied virtue until we experience it through an epiphany, a sudden intuitive leap of understanding. Amy thought she understood the virtue of compassion. It wasn't until she witnessed her father become confused in his own kitchen that she truly comprehended its meaning.

***Applied virtue has the power to take hold of us and change our perceptions. This is the third property of applied virtue.*** Meilaender writes of virtues, "they influence how we describe the activities in which we engage, what we think we are doing, and what we think important about what we are doing . . . Our virtues do not just simply fit us for life; they help shape life."

When perception shifts, so does life. I often promote my coaching practice by saying I "sell" new observations, new ways of perceiving events and situations. When I am privileged to watch someone reach a moment of illumination—a flash of understanding when they see with new eyes—I am deeply satisfied. Once the veil is removed, there is no going back. The person in front of me has changed, forever.

The application of virtue alters how we perceive our circumstances. This new interpretation, in turn, amends our use of language. Naturally, the words we choose will reflect our new mindset. But the power of virtue doesn't stop there. It also transforms our bodies. Where frustration might have caused frantic or violent movement, applied virtue produces smooth, graceful motions and gestures.

As for Amy, her perceptions of her father were outdated ones. As the virtue of compassion took hold again, she began to see Aron differently. Amy realized he was much more and much less than the superhuman hero she had always imagined him to be. Supported by virtue, Amy's gestures became softer, less rough. Her voice lightened and the light came back to her eyes.

*Applied virtue arises from a purposeful selection between two options: the virtuous path and the status quo.* All of us have the potential to be listed among the ranks of the virtuous. What separates us from people such as Mother Teresa, the Dalai Lama, and Gandhi is not physical distance, opportunity, or time, but the choices we make.

When it comes to asking for help, many of us would rather take the easy way out, retain the status quo, and not make the request at all. We reason that it would be simpler to handle things on our own. We assure ourselves that it would be too much effort for someone else to get involved, or that we might be asking for trouble! Our petty worries convince us that it would be easier to struggle on alone.

Choosing to go it alone isn't always the best choice. In fact, choosing to involve another may just be the virtuous option left unexplored.

Have you read the book or seen the film version of *To Kill a Mockingbird*? Attorney Atticus Finch, the beloved father of Scout and Jem, was a truly virtuous man. He had many opportunities throughout the story to choose the easy way out, to choose not to represent a black man falsely accused of rape. Atticus, a man whom virtue had already changed, never flinched when he selected the hard road and did the right thing.

Another example, based on an unfortunate reality, is the action of the passengers of United Airlines Flight 93, that crashed into a Pennsylvania field on September 11, 2001. Their deliberate choice to rush the hijackers served as an example to every American. Their individual honor and collective courage cost them their futures, but that act saved the lives of thousands of others. A great deal of virtue was exhibited that day. The inhumane cruelty of Al Qaeda affected us all, but the grand and small virtuous acts that day reminded us of what we could be and changed us for the better.

It might seem that resolving a need on your own is actually the more difficult choice—after all, you are the one doing the work. Not quite. Asking for aid, inviting another into our troubled life, resurrects our greatest fears of separation, shame, and surrender. It forces us to risk on an emotional level, not an intellectual one. Choosing virtue demands more of you, more of your spirit. Asking for help is, indeed, the harder choice.

## Applying Virtue to Asking for Help

With these four properties, virtue becomes useful, within reach, and easily applicable. These "emotions on steroids" can be applied in a myriad of situations, whether at home, at work, or at the ball field. That goes for asking for help, too.

Trifling fear prohibits us from asking for what we need. It motivates us to stay with the status quo, the known, our usual habits. If we are to reach out and receive the benefits of making a mayday call, other more powerful emotional states are demanded. Applied virtue is required.

**TRY THIS**   EXPLORING VIRTUE

Virtue is a concept that few of us think about on a regular basis, but it is worth examining. Answer the following questions to get reacquainted with the power of virtue.

- Who are the people you admire most in life? (They can be living or dead.) What virtuous qualities do they possess?

- How do you think they learned to be so virtuous? What were their personal epiphanies? If you don't know, it might be worth investigating.

- How do you think these virtues changed their lives?

Shifting away from fear, we open ourselves to the transformative power of applied virtue. Our perceptions about asking for help will change. We no longer see it as an intimidating process, a step of last resort. With applied virtue, everything that seemed impossible is now possible, even likely.

In this part, you've examined what stops us from asking for what we need. You've also discovered the wonderful blessings that come when we reach out and ask for that helping hand. And you've been introduced to the underpinnings of the *Mayday!* process: anchoring principles, seed emotions, and applied virtues. In Part Two, you will read about the specific steps of the process and the role that applied virtue plays in making your requests for help clear, strong, and centered.

# PART 2

# THE
# MAYDAY!
## PROCESS

# THE MAYDAY! PROCESS

| Name the need | Give yourself a break | Take a leap | Ask! | Be grateful | Listen differently | Say thanks |
|---|---|---|---|---|---|---|
| **BEFORE THE REQUEST** | | **DURING THE REQUEST** | | **AFTER THE REQUEST** | | |

# STEP 1

# NAME THE NEED

∎∎∎ ▬ ▬ ▬ ∎∎∎

A man travels the world over
in search of what he needs
and returns home to find it.
*George Moore*

In 2005, disaster struck New Orleans. Hurricane Katrina hit the Gulf Coast and battered the Crescent City until there was practically nothing left. Flooding forced people to their roofs where they signaled to passing helicopters. Day after day, thousands of people cried out: *Help*!

Months before Katrina, a tsunami hit Indonesia killing thousands. Entire communities were destroyed. More than 212,000 people were swept away or killed by debris. Homes gone, infrastructure gone, and thousands of families torn apart.

Clearly, the victims of these catastrophes experienced grave fear, fear for their lives and for the lives of their loved ones. It's not difficult to guess the immediate needs of the residents of New Orleans and Indonesia. None of us even needed to see the horrendous scenes on television, we knew instinctively what was required to help those poor souls: water, food, safety, and housing.

Thankfully, most of our crises are not so vast. They can be filled quickly and without the massive marshaling of troops and international support services. When it comes to asking for help, determining and defining the need are not so easily accomplished. *The very nature of being in need keeps us in the dark and discourages us from exploring unknown pathways or novel approaches to fulfillment of our needs. Occasionally, what we think we need is not what we need at all.*

## Step 1: Name the Need

The very first step of the *Mayday!* process is focused on defining your need. When we feel the nervous angst of an unresolved problem, we want to eliminate that feeling almost immediately. We can't wait to get it fixed fast enough. This is a natural first reaction. However, this step of the *Mayday!* process requires us to slow down and ask some questions. The intent is to get as clear about the need as possible and, at the same time, remain open to other possibilities. The following questions will move you toward clarity and openness.

### What are your personal distress signals?

Sometimes when I don't know I need help, others around me do know. They see me acting stressed and even out of control. Over time, I have learned to notice most of the warning signs, my personal distress signals. We all have them, and your friends, like mine, may perceive them before you do. These personal distress signals are designed to grab our attention and get us to acknowledge that we can't do it on our own.

For example, you may notice an internal nervousness that

resists being soothed. Maybe you have been more impatient than usual or perhaps your mood swings are fairly dramatic. Possibly, panic has found a way of creeping in at the start of your days, just before things get moving. Or maybe the anxiety captures you at night, just as you curl up in bed. Perhaps you experience crushing bouts of dissatisfaction with your current life and/or general pessimism about your future. You might even feel as though you are riding a giant pendulum, causing your emotions to swing from one side to the other.

Perhaps you've lost sleep because you wake up in the middle of the night, or you can't drop off in the first place. Maybe your usual eating habits have changed for the worse. Did today's lunch consist of microwaved popcorn noshed between appointments? You might have noticed a few more headaches. Perhaps, you can't stop yawning—not because you are sleepy, but because you don't seem to be able to get enough air. As for working out, forget it. And, of course, you don't have to admit it to anyone, but maybe your libido just isn't what it used to be.

There's a chance too, that you seem to be whining more than usual. All you notice is what's wrong, never what's right. Maybe that's something that your partner has pointed out—numerous times. The things that never used to bother you now send you into a rage. That voice in your head never gives you a break, as though its switch is stuck on auto-repeat. Perhaps too, you can't seem to remember anything or keep your mind on the task in front of you. Maybe you've become so focused on the details you can't see the big picture anymore, or vice versa.

Your body, mind, and emotions are trying to get your attention. These emotional, physical, and mental sensations are your personal distress signals—the warning signs that something is out of whack. With your mind on your problems, you might not see these signals at all—even if to others they seem like flashing strobe lights. These symptoms may have become such a regular part everyday of your life that they appear normal to you.

Do your shoulders feel tight, or your lower back knot up? Perhaps you are carrying too much of a load and you just need a little help with your burdens. Does your head hurt? Maybe you've been over-analyzing things; perhaps you need help finding time to play. Have you noticed that you've been grinding your teeth or that you regularly clamp your jaws shut? Perhaps you have wanted to tell someone something for a while and you need help getting the message across. The body doesn't lie. We might be able to convince our minds and those around us that we'll be all right, but the body knows better. It's not going to let you get away with the overwork, the overstress, the doing it alone. Your body is going to send you signals until you do something about the help you need.

**TRY THIS    NOTICING YOUR OWN DISTRESS SIGNALS**

Remember back to a time when you wanted to cry Mayday! What were the personal distress signals that let you know you needed help?

♦ What happened to your forehead when you were puzzling over a problem?

♦ What happened to your voice? Did it get higher pitched, lower, louder, softer?

♦ What happened to your jaw? Did it tighten or clamp down?

♦ What happened to your shoulders or upper back? Did they tighten up?

♦ What do you do with your hands? Did you shake them, bite your nails, drum your fingers, or crack your knuckles?

♦ What happened to the pace of your heart? Did it speed up or slow down?

- What happened to your breathing? Did it become shallow, deeper, slower, or faster?

- What happened to your overall posture? Did you slump over or stand tall?

- What happened to your eating habits? Did you eat more? Less?

- What happened to your exercise regimen? Did it increase or decrease?

- What happened to your relationships? Did they go through a "rough patch?"

"It will pass," is a common phrase. Instead of seeing these behaviors and actions as indicators that something is wrong, we perceive them as annoyances or inconveniences. We are all smart enough to know that sometimes these symptoms won't just "pass." The body, mind, and emotions will return to balance only when we face our needs and deal with them.

## What Is Your First Guess?

Once we notice our own personal distress, we instinctively take a guess at the best solution to our problem. This natural, almost instantaneous, reaction makes sense—we are thinkers. We live mostly in our heads. Our minds are rarely at rest, so they often go into overdrive when a need presents itself.

In business today, it's common for a manager to warn her staff, "Don't come to me with a problem unless you know how to solve it." This admonition was originally created to lessen the burden on management and to encourage independent thought within the ranks of the workforce. On the one hand, the warning can be helpful. On the other hand, if a solution isn't apparent, this same caution can send us spiraling toward the fear of shame. "How can I go to her with this problem? She'll think I'm stupid for letting it happen and even more stupid because I don't know how to solve it."

Not only that, but when our distress signals are active, our thoughts are usually muddled because the riptide of fear is pulling for control. Fear does nothing to promote creativity of thought. Instead it crushes inspiration before it has a chance to start. Creative problem solving is best achieved when our heads are clear, when our bodies are calm, and when our emotions are optimistic. I don't know about you, but when I'm struggling with an issue, the images in my mind blast through at a rapid pace. My body refuses to relax and my emotions head toward the dark side. In this state, I'll never generate the ideas I need to release me from my dilemma.

Remember, fear, by its very nature, seeks to deceive. All fears try to convince us that the status quo is better than moving into the unknown. It doesn't want us to see the possibilities that exist just beyond our sight. When we experience fear, no matter what kind, that list of possibilities is immediately restricted. We see only what fear wants us to see.

So before you ask for the help you need, remind yourself that your suggested resolution is only that, a suggestion. Your helpmate may have a much better idea.

Allan, a small business owner, was reeling from a market downturn. His revenues had dropped substantially, and he worried that he would have to begin laying off his employees. Over the years, Allan had created a support group of men and women who were also running their own small businesses. He knew they weren't doing any better than he was. Each month, they would meet for breakfast and commiserate about the state of the economy. Each month, Allan would walk away feeling even more depressed and downhearted.

Allan came to me, asking me to help him find a way to invigorate his business. I answered, "It seems to me that what you need right now is a new support group, not a new business plan."

Confused, Allan listened as I explained that his continued focus on what was missing in his business could be the real problem. Having an informal monthly pity-party wasn't helping. It wasn't much of a *support* group if he felt lousy afterward. Perhaps what he needed was a new set of voices and ideas. "Perhaps what you need every month is something or someone to inspire you to go back to your office with a better attitude and optimistic outlook."

"That makes sense," he replied. "If all I ever notice is what I don't have, I won't pay attention to any of the good things I do have." Allan went back to his office determined to remain confident and upbeat. He found new people to listen to. He cut back on his breakfasts with the old crowd. It seemed to do the trick. His business rebounded well before anyone else's on his "support" team.

Allan's first guess at what he needed was a good one, but it wasn't the right one. So deep in his need, Allan couldn't see any other option than to change his business strategy. No matter how much he changed his strategy, his attitude would still have gotten in the way.

How many times have you confused what you want with what you need? How many times have you insisted that you knew exactly what had to happen in order for you to get your needs met? How many times have you subsequently realized that maybe what you thought you needed wasn't really necessary? Your first solution is only one of many possibilities. Do not believe that because you came up with it, it is the only or the best solution.

## Am I Attached to the Solution?

It is not unusual for us to become attached to our first guess. We decide that this solution is the one and only one that will get us the results we want. Insisting that we know what is best may be shortsighted and could limit our discovery of other creative solutions.

"Unattachment is the release of need or expectation associated with a specific outcome," notes Cherie Carter-Scott in her book *If Life Is a Game, These Are the Rules.* "We become attached to the way we envision something working out, and struggle to make circumstances bend to our desires. Life, however, often has its own agenda, and we are destined to suffer unless we give up our attachment to things working out exactly as we would like." If we truly need help, then we may be suffering already. Why add more anguish to the situation by forcing a conclusion?

Maggie and Colin were having troubles in their marriage. Maggie was sure they needed counseling, but Colin resisted it. Maggie just couldn't let go of the idea that an experienced counselor would provide the help they needed to better understand each other. Colin, on the other hand, thought they could work it out themselves. The fears of surrender and shame nagged at him. He didn't like the idea of involving an unfamiliar person in their marriage, and he certainly didn't want anyone to think they couldn't solve their own problems. Long arguments ensued over which solution was the best. They needed help.

One afternoon, while they were visiting Colin's family, Maggie sat down with Colin's mother. The two women got to talking about Colin and his particular style of communicating. Unbeknownst to Maggie, Colin was, at the same time, talking with his brother. Maggie and Colin were quiet on the ride home. Settling down for the evening, they slowly began to talk to each other. The insight they received from Colin's mother and brother was enough to break the impasse they had created. Maggie realized that wisdom can arrive in very different forms, and Colin understood that an additional perspective can prove valuable.

Part of Maggie's and Colin's difficulty came from their attachment to their original choices for help. Maggie believed wholeheartedly that counseling was the way to go; Colin thought that they already had the tools they needed to resolve their differences. Neither was true.

Maggie and Colin missed seeing how their attachment to different resolutions was creating new problems. Those who answer your cry for help are capable adults accustomed to making decisions and living full and productive lives, just like you. They don't need to be told what to do and they don't usually respond well if you do. Now is not the appropriate time to remain resolute, especially when you are under the spell of the riptides. Respect your helpmate's experience and strength. You'll get more commitment and support if you remain open to new possibilities.

## What Is the Gap?

As technical as it might sound, a gap analysis will also help you narrow down your specific need. A management tool used in many different disciplines including skill development and business assessment, gap analysis is simply a comparison of the current state with the desired future state. If our current situation is unacceptable, we assume that there is a better way, a better existence. The gap is that space between what is and what is better. That is the need that we seek help with.

Juan was an artist trapped in the body and life of a construction foreman. His dream was to spend his days working in his studio, watching the light fall on live models and painting until night arrived. But Juan also had responsibilities to his family and to his employer. He came to me seeking counsel because his boss had just offered him a promotion. Normally considered a good thing, Juan didn't want this upgrade. "It will mean more time on the road, more time dealing with personnel issues, more time away from what I love doing," he explained.

Juan had a need. A gap existed between what he wanted— a life of beauty and artistry—and what he had—a life devoted to contractors and blueprints. The question now, was how to close the gap?

We began by prioritizing the important elements of his life. Here is his list:

1. My family

2. My employer

3. Me, my painting

Juan's gap analysis clearly defined the current situation and his desired future state. With his three priorities, it became easy for the two of us to brainstorm a solution. At first, Juan was pretty sure he'd lose his job if he refused the promotion. After some discussion, he realized that was the fear of separation talking. He knew he was a great asset to the company and that his boss would be crazy to let him go. So Juan went to his boss and asked him for help keeping his life intact. He explained that the new role was not what he wanted. To soften the blow, Juan offered to find someone to fill the new position. "You should have seen his face when I said no to the promotion. But, then you should have seen mine afterward. I was so relieved." Juan achieved his goal of supporting his family by continuing in his role as foreman. He may not have fully satisfied his employer, but Juan continued to be an effective site leader. This gave him time to continue to paint and to satisfy his need for creativity.

**TRY THIS    WHAT IS YOUR GAP?**

♦ Describe the situation as you see it. What are problems this situation is causing you or about to cause you?

♦ Describe the ideal scenario. What would be different?

♦ What are your priorities?

♦ Now, record your first guess at how to best resolve your issue.

## Do I Have a Need or a Want?

Now that you've explored the gap, ask yourself one more question: Is this what I need or what I want? The dictionaries provide a variety of definitions for both *need* and *want*, but here's a good shorthand description: A need is something that you have to have, a want is something that you'd like to have. A need is a requirement, a want is an option. The definitions are simple to understand but not always so simple to apply.

Consider Juan's situation. Some would read his story and think he had it all wrong. Choosing to paint instead of earning more money for his family sounds like Juan put his wants over his needs. For Juan, painting is a need. He wasn't a dabbler. No, he felt a compulsion to pick up a brush every day. He was financially stable and his wife earned a good income. Money wasn't the issue, satisfying his creativity was. For Juan, the choice was the right one.

In working with Juan, we could have used Maslow's *Hierarchy of Needs*. In the 1940s, noted psychologist Abraham Maslow identified a range of needs from the lowest, such as food, water, and breathing, to the highest level of personal self-actualization. Juan had achieved the basics: physiological needs, safety, love/belonging, and self-esteem. Now, it was time for him to focus on self-actualization.

# HIERARCHY OF NEEDS

SELF-ACTUALIZATION

SELF-ESTEEM

BELONGING

SAFETY

PHYSIOLOGICAL NEEDS

Abraham Maslow, 1943
"A Theory of Human Motivation"

**TRY THIS   IS IT A NEED OR A WANT?**

As you consider the gap, distinguish between *need* and *want*. Spend time thinking about this, not just reacting to the itch to resolve it. Ask yourself:

♦ Have I taken care of other more urgent needs? (Those at the bottom of the model.)

♦ Is the help I seek necessary for me and my loved ones to be healthy and safe?

♦ How long could I go without it?

♦ Will having it make me feel better about myself?

♦ Can I achieve that another way?

♦ What are the consequences of not getting this need resolved?

♦ How will those consequences affect me and those I love?

If you suspect that the help you seek is "nice to have," then treat it that way. Ask for help in satisfying it, and at the same time, understand that your *want* is ultimately less important than your *need*. Do your best to avoid behaving as though fulfillment of your desire is critical. Those who answer your mayday calls will want to know whether they are working toward fulfilling a requirement or an option.

We can be so hard on ourselves. What if we gave ourselves permission *not to know* how to solve everything? If it were that easy to think our way out of problems, don't you think we would have already? What if we remained open to other suggestions, other ways of meeting our needs? The burden would shift from one set of shoulders to at least two. Go ahead and take a guess, but remember, it is only a guess.

# GIVE YOURSELF A BREAK

∎∎∎━━━∎∎∎

If you want others to be happy, practice compassion.
If you want to be happy, practice compassion.
*The Dalai Lama*

The *Mayday!* process has begun. At this point, you see the
gap between what you have and what you need. You might
even feel this disparity acutely. You have an idea of how the
need could be met but have decided to remain open to other
options. There is a strong possibility that fear still holds you
back from obtaining the gifts of flow and connection that
come from asking for help. It's as though fear jams your personal frequencies, stopping you from making any kind of
mayday call. Now is the time to take another deep breath and
to move on to Step 2.

## Step 2: Give Yourself a Break, Practice Compassion

It is damn difficult living life in this day and age. We face
complexities and challenges that our ancestors couldn't even

begin to imagine. We are inundated with messages about how we should be, what we should buy, which groups we should belong to. Our minds are rarely at peace. We think constantly. We schedule our days, jamming them with more than we could ever possibly accomplish in twenty-four hours. Our bodies work overtime trying to squeeze "it" all in. And, to complicate matters, we have others to consider, too. We work to make sure they are provided with all they need. We involve our loved ones in almost all our major decisions. And through it all, there is very little room for us. When do we get a little "me" time? Who cares for the caregiver? Step 2 is all about breaking away from our relentless focus on everything and everyone else. *To send out our mayday signals, we need to believe it is permissible to ask for help.* That's where the applied virtue of compassion comes into play.

## The Applied Virtue of Compassion

Let's assume you need help right now. Hopefully, you've vowed that your worries are not going to get the better of you this time. Just then, a little voice inside your head says, "Who am I to ask for help? My problems are so minor compared to others. Everyone else is so busy anyway." Okay, so maybe you aren't as ready as you thought . . . yet. That's because the first applied virtue, compassion—specifically compassion for *you*—is not in place.

Just as the three riptides of fear (surrender, separation, and shame) begin their lies with a seed of truth, the applied virtues also begin with something small, an emotional seed. The emotional seed of the virtue of compassion is *sympathy*.

*Sympathy*, according to *Merriam-Webster's Dictionary*, is "an affinity, association, or relationship between persons or things wherein whatever affects one similarly affects the other." A sameness of feeling, an understanding of someone's suffering, sympathy is a passive emotion. The actions it produces are less demonstrative, more reserved. When we are sympathetic to someone's situation, we nod our heads in recognition of their trial and we may shed a tear or two. We may sit and hold a hand or "be there" for someone. These small actions can provide comfort to the target of our sympathy. But sympathy, in and of itself, does not compel us to great acts. But combine it with another element and it can change into a powerful force, an applied virtue.

Four years ago, Kathleen made what I thought was a difficult and courageous choice. She quit her job as an attorney at a prestigious law firm in downtown Chicago and moved to Bolivia to work in a children's orphanage.

Kathleen began her emotional journey with deep sympathy after hearing stories about these children. She couldn't get the memory of them out of her head or her heart. After months of experiencing the ineffectiveness of this passive emotional state, she realized that she needed more! The kids needed more! Kathleen felt compelled to act, to combine her sympathy with a desire to do something for these children.

Kathleen first embraced the seed emotion of *sympathy*. She kept it alive and evolving. When she made a deliberate decision to act, to blend her life with theirs, the AV of compassion became firmly embedded in her heart. It was her active compassion for those neglected children that caused her to give up everything and care for them.

*Compassion*, according to *Merriam-Webster's*, is a "sympathetic consciousness of others' distress together with a desire to alleviate it." Note the key distinction here: *sympathy* helps us recognize suffering, but *compassion* moves us to alleviate it. With *sympathy* we can relate to the anguish, but *compassion* leads us to share and transform it.

**Sympathy + A Desire to Act = Compassion**

Compassion is what moves us to help others in need. Sympathy and the AV of compassion may also be applied during our own times of need, when we would do well to ask for help. Instead of directing those feelings toward others, however, we must aim them at ourselves!

## The Applied Virtue of Self-Compassion

While holding great compassion for the orphans, Kathleen had reserved very little for herself. She had spent two months getting ready for her move to South America. She had subleased her apartment and made arrangements to access her finances while out of the country. Orchestrating her own going-away party, Kathleen combined it with a drive to accept donated socks and underwear for the Bolivian children she'd be living with. She had spent weeks saying goodbye to friends and family. So concerned with everyone and everything else, Kathleen had forgotten about her own needs.

The breaking point came when Kathleen was to board a plane in less than twenty-four hours, but she had yet to pack a box or move her belongings into storage. Pushed to the brink, Kathleen now found herself stressed and in tears. She needed help herself but couldn't find the words to ask for it. In a conversation months later, she admitted that she had not felt justified in asking others to give of their weekend time to help her . . . as though our free time meant more than helping a dear friend!

A mayday call went out from a mutual friend who had guessed that Kathleen was struggling to get it all done in time. Once phone calls were made, six of us arrived on her doorstep to fold clothes, pack books, and tape boxes shut. In a few hours, her belongings were packed and ready to be loaded into a waiting van.

The AV of *self*-compassion also begins with the seed emotion of sympathy, which is too weak to create the bold move Kathleen needed to take: to ask for help. Directed inwardly, sympathy results in actions such as silent wishes and deep sighs. Like all seed emotions, sympathy doesn't produce bold steps. However, if we combine the seed of sympathy with an added ingredient, a desire to alleviate our own suffering, then we can conjure the AV of self-compassion.

### Sympathy + A Desire to Act on One's Own Behalf = Self-Compassion

Kathleen didn't feel right asking for a helping hand. If she had been supported by the AV of self-compassion, she would have asked for help from those who love her.

*There is a hidden message within the powerful emotional state. The AV of self-compassion reminds you that you are justified in asking for help.* Why? Because you are a human being with intrinsic worth and value. You are a child of the Universe, equal to any other, as deserving as any other. Because you love and are loved, you merit all that asking for help has to offer.

Any time you "cut yourself a little slack" or "give yourself a break," you are using self-compassion. Perhaps a co-worker has suggested that you might be a bit "too hard on yourself." This is a sign that you might be in need of a little—or a lot of—self-compassion. Or perhaps you have driven yourself to exhaustion. What if you slowed yourself down and injected a little personal compassion into your life instead? You might discover that a little self-care goes a long way.

**TRY THIS**   S E L F - C O M P A S S I O N

How does self-compassion show up in your life? Answer the questions and see.

♦ Describe a time when you didn't cut yourself the slack you deserved. Why didn't you?

♦ Describe a time when you did give yourself a break. Why did you?

♦ What was different about these two situations?


## Self-Compassion and the Great Fears

It's funny how some people react when we exhibit self-compassion or self-care. About the time I began to learn about the benefits of asking for help, I made a decision to get rid of some of the household chores that were sapping my energy. I registered for a grocery delivery service and hired a housecleaner. I even began to look for a personal chef to prepare and freeze meals every week. This freed me up to do things that were more meaningful and fun.

I shared with Joey, an acquaintance, my plan to "outsource" a lot of these kinds of household tasks. He looked straight into my eyes and said, "I'm surprised you feel as though you need to do that. Isn't that a bit lazy?" I was stunned at his rude assessment of my choice. It's not unusual, unfortunately. Joey is no different from others who equate self-care with laziness or selfishness. In his eyes, I should have been embarrassed for being so lazy. Joey was the one who was afraid of shame, not me.

Fears of surrender, separation, and shame diminish to the point of powerlessness when we adopt the applied virtue of self-compassion. Virtue trumps fear because its truth originates in spirit, not ego. Self-compassion leaves no room for the ego to spout its lies. Instead, it fills us with peace. It reminds us that we are worthy. It lets us know that we deserve to ask for help.

When the fear of separation insidiously whispers, "You will lose what you love if you ask for help," the applied virtue of self-compassion counters, "Those who truly love and know me will help." When fear snickers that you are alone, the AV of self-compassion declares, "I may not know who, but someone will help."

The AV of self-compassion also silences the lies propagated by the fear of shame. I was able to let Joey's concerns bounce right off me because I knew and believed that asking for help is the right thing to do. With self-compassion, you will feel the same.

Finally, self-compassion dispels the fear of surrender. It encourages us to let go of ego and surrender ourselves to the care of others. The ego hates this idea. It doesn't want you to experience the feeling of shelter and security in the caring arms of another. Self-compassion gives us permission to surrender to the talents, creativity and genius of our chosen helpmates.

## THE APPLIED VIRTUE MATRIX

| Applied Virtue | Definition | The Emotional Seed | Combined with | The Hidden Message |
|---|---|---|---|---|
| Compassion | A desire to alleviate the suffering of others | Sympathy: an understanding of another's suffering | A desire to act on behalf of someone else | Others are deserving of help |
| Self-Compassion | A desire to alleviate our own suffering | Sympathy: an understanding of our own suffering | A desire to act on one's own behalf | You are deserving of help |

## Self-Compassion's Effect on our Bodies and Minds

The reciprocal action between emotion/body and language is essential to the *Mayday!* process. As you adopt any of the applied virtues, your language and physical presence will reflect these new and powerful emotional states. In turn, your mayday signals will reflect these same positive feelings.

At the moment you experience self-compassion, you will notice, if you pay attention, physical changes. Your breathing will deepen and become more uniform. You might even release a sigh of relief. Nervous energy will immediately begin to dissipate.

With self-compassion, you will feel somehow softer. Anytime you struggle to make it all work, to get everything done, to fulfill every need, your body prepares for the onslaught of activity. It becomes rigid, like a suit of armor designed to support and protect you. With too much use, the armor can become a cage. If you choose to be self-compassionate, your protective covering loses its inflexibility. Where there was stiffness, there is now a gentle softness. Your muscles loosen and your hands unclench. You might even feel the muscles around your eyes relaxing. A scowl or knitted brow will be replaced with an understanding smile.

In addition to changing you physically, self-compassion also transforms your words. A peaceful knowingness accompanies self-compassion. Previous beliefs about who you are and what you need no longer have relevance. You now see yourself differently: not as someone who needs to be protected, but as someone seeking flow, connection, and love. Your inner chatter changes, too. "I don't want to bother anyone," becomes "It is time I allowed myself some help." Your language and word choice become less abusive and more caring. Instead of "lazy," you'll refer to yourself as "deserving." You will emphatically agree that it's high time you gave yourself a break. Any mayday signal you send at this point will accurately represent your conviction that you deserve to ask for help and all the treasures it has to offer.

## Acting from Self-Compassion

What happens when we apply the AV of self-compassion to our lives? We breathe and relax knowing we deserve to make our mayday calls. We decide to ask for the help we need. We exhibit self-care.

The AV of self-compassion moves you toward your furthest potentialities by causing you to act deliberately on your own behalf. With compassion for yourself, you instinctively ask for the help you need.

Just as compassion alleviates the suffering of others, compassion for ourselves enables us to ease our own anguish and to lovingly care for ourselves. This is self-care, not to be confused with selfishness. Selfish people focus on their own needs to the exclusion of others. Pure selfishness is a rare phenomenon. Instead, what seems more common is self-neglect. So concerned with others we ignore, sometimes quite cruelly, our own suffering. Self-compassion does not give you permission to ignore another's pain; it does gives you permission to pay attention to your own.

## Learning Self-Compassion

At first, the AV of self-compassion may feel unfamiliar, even uncomfortable. The ego will react and tell you that you are being self-centered. With discipline and a little practice, you can begin to realize the tender rewards described in Chapter 3. Simplicity, flow, and connection can all be yours . . . just for the asking.

I finally got the lesson about self-care that my friends had tried to teach me over many years. It became clear to me what I was doing to myself when I refused to apply a little self-compassion and take it easy on myself.

During a guided visualization, an image came to me that was startling. In my mind's eye, I saw a young boy walking, really limping, toward me from a nearby grove of trees. Dressed in rags, he walked with the help of a makeshift crutch. As he moved closer, I could see how badly hurt he was. His face and skinny little arms were covered in dirt and bruises. A little blood was encrusted on his forehead.

I was shocked at the abuse he had taken. I felt intense compassion for this little boy. He crawled into my lap, placing his head just over my heart. I put my arms around him.

"Who did this to you?" I asked.

"You did," he replied.

I was taken aback, and even in a meditative state, I could feel my breath become shallow. (I feel it even now.) I asked, "What? How is that possible?"

This little boy raised his face to mine—I could barely look at him—and he explained, "Anytime you decided not to accept the help of another, anytime you refused to care for yourself, anytime you neglected your own spirit, I was injured. These are the bruises of years of futile effort and needless isolation."

My epiphany. The meaning of self-compassion was made real to me in that visualization.

This little boy, whom I later named Bruised Bobby, represented the innocent and powerless part of my psyche. It had never occurred to me that each time I chose self-sufficiency over self-care I was injuring part of myself. Every rejected opportunity was recorded on this little guy's broken body. Bobby was certainly deserving of better care, and seeing this, I realized I was too.

You have your own version of Bruised Bobby. You may not have met him yet, but he's there. Each time you refuse the virtue of self-compassion, you do harm to yourself.

Conjure your own inner child. Spend some time medi-
tating on the existence of that little boy or girl and the lessons he or she has to teach you about self-compassion. Ask
yourself, "Do I not deserve better care? As an adult, am I really any different than the child inside me? Don't I deserve to
be cared for and helped?"

**TRY THIS    LEARNING TO BE SELF-COMPASSIONATE**

Try out these approaches to acquiring and practicing self-compassion:

◆ Look at your needs compared to the needs of others whom you have
helped in the past. Ask yourself, "Is my situation really any less deserving of attention?"

◆ Hire a housecleaner or a grocery delivery service or some other service you might consider a luxury. If you find yourself resisting, ask
yourself, "Don't I deserve to be pampered?" It's important not to
go to an extreme here; you don't want to overextend yourself financially. But allowing an indulgence every once in a while is a self-compassionate thing to do.

◆ Whenever you exercise or go for a walk, repeat a mantra to yourself.
The combination of *body* movement and *language* mantra will help
shift your emotional state toward self-compassion. Use the following or make up your own: "I have needs that I cannot meet alone. I
need and deserve help."

◆ Stick a picture of yourself as a child on your refrigerator. Every time
you look at it, remind yourself that there is still, within you, a child
looking to be cared for.

## Changing Perceptions with the AV of Self-Compassion

The AV of self-compassion alters our perceptions, changing
how we view the world. Instead of seeing life as a battle or a
race—two common metaphors—we can look at it as a journey of exploration and growth. Instead of trying to achieve
specific goals by a certain age, in effect, pushing for control,

self-compassion returns us to the flow. Rather than manage everything around us, self-compassion encourages us to surrender to the mysterious magic of life.

Our world becomes different with self-compassion. Days become long enough; we find the time to squeeze in small acts of self-care like relaxing vacations, golf games, and massages. We find it's possible to get to the gym or go for a run. We stop working on the weekends. We schedule time to think and to just be. Interruptions no longer annoy us, instead we see them as chances to break away for a moment, opportunities to be involved in another's life.

Our compassion for others deepens, too. As we learn to recognize the signs of our own distress, we begin to notice those same signals in those around us. With these new eyes, we encourage others to take a break or we offer help.

With self-compassion we no longer worry about whether or not we should ask for help. Of course we should!

## The Choice: The AV of Self-Compassion

*A mindful choice is required to generate all applied virtues, including self-compassion.* Just like me, you've probably already tried doing it all on your own. That isn't working, is it? The status quo—doing it alone—hasn't turned out so well. Perhaps it is time for you to activate self-compassion; to choose between what you have always done, habits of work and interaction that no longer serve you, and something new and unfamiliar, a chance to alleviate your own suffering.

Adopting the AV of self-compassion, life suddenly becomes easier, and the decision we agonized over no longer seems so hard. Cutting yourself a break brings you a softer existence, one that's not built with the rigidity of self-sufficiency. No longer feeling as though you have to do it all, and do it all well, you find yourself within the flow of life.

Remember, being in the flow is easy, being out of it is what makes life hard. Choosing to be self-compassionate takes you back to the river.

The unhappy reality is that many of us do go to that place of desperation before we are able to choose self-compassion. Sometimes we have to break down before we see how hard we've been on ourselves.

Let's finish Amy's story from Chapter 4. Her father had developed symptoms of severe dementia and Amy had chosen, quite unselfishly, to care for him during this awful time. But Amy went a little too far in her efforts to help her father. Along the way, she completely forgot about caring for herself. She felt excruciatingly guilty whenever she thought about leaving him to go out with friends. Between work and caring for her father, Amy had exhausted herself.

I had suggested to her that she deserved a little time to herself. Amy fought the suggestion, believing that caring for her father was her responsibility alone, and that leaving him was tantamount to abandonment. Our conversation was wholly unsatisfying to Amy. I didn't hear from her for a long time after that. Finally, she called and told me what happened.

Amy visited her storage unit one day to retrieve an item. She was caught off guard by the mementos and belongings she had locked away. They reminded her of the life she had left behind. These memories caused an emotional shift within her. She swung from guilt and self-recrimination to one of possibility and self-compassion.

She explained, "Something about seeing all my belongings—I realized that I had put way too much pressure on myself. It suddenly occurred to me that I couldn't go on like this anymore. I had to do something different. I had to find help for me and for my dad."

The next morning Amy started looking for help. She began by calling someone she barely knew, a woman who was in a similar situation. By the end of the call, Amy had a list of resources and services that catered to families of Alzheimer patients. She even found one church-based organization that offered free care for two to four hours a week. This was perfect for Amy. It gave her enough time to pamper herself and relax. None of this would have happened had Amy not shifted toward self-compassion and understood that she deserved care as much as her father did.

## Applying Self-Compassion to Asking for Help

Let's put it all together. At this point in the *Mayday!* process you see a gap between what your current state is and what you'd like it to be. You've spent some time clarifying, as best you can, what your need is. Now, it's time to generate enough self-compassion for yourself so that you truly believe, in your bones, that you deserve to send out a mayday signal—to ask for help.

**TRY THIS**   **WHY YOU DESERVE HELP**

♦ Write a letter to yourself. As you write, imagine you are your best friend or closest buddy. From his or her perspective, write why you deserve the help you seek.

♦ Now write a short note, from yourself, in response. In your note, commit to making a mayday call.

When you invite applied virtue into your life, things change. The applied virtue of self-compassion changes you physically, softening you, leaving you open and vulnerable. At the same time, self-compassion changes the way you view your world. It moves you away from believing that you are less worthy than others of receiving a gift of help. It directs you toward a vision that will liberate you so you can experience flow, simplicity, personal growth, and deeper connection with those around you.

Self-compassion moves you to act on your own behalf, to take that step that your loved ones want you to take, to ask for help.

## Gina's Story of Self-Compassion

Gina learned to apply the virtue of self-compassion to her life, but only after much anguish. A young mother with an out-of-work husband, Gina found herself supporting her family not just financially, but emotionally as well. She was also newly promoted to a position of great responsibility within her company. Gina was under great pressure as many people were relying on her.

For the past year she spent her energy focusing on her son, her husband, and her direct reports, neglecting herself in the process. She put on weight, started to smoke again, and weakly suppressed her own depression that had begun to take root soon after her husband lost his job. Gina felt very much alone and abandoned by the world.

I met Gina just as she was about to fall apart. Her supervisor called me in to speak with her, and in our first session together it became clear to me that, in addition to coaching, Gina needed professional psychological care.

In our first meeting, I learned what terrified Gina and how little compassion she had for herself. First, she was afraid of failing at work. How could she take time off to deal with anything when so many others were relying on her (fear of surrender)? In addition, she felt pressure to perform (fear of shame), and she was sure she'd never get another promotion, given how badly her current performance level was. In fact she was worried that she might lose her job (fear of separation).

Second, Gina believed that her needs were secondary to those of her toddler son and struggling husband. And the company culture also promoted the idea that the team must always come first. There was no room for Gina and her problems in this scenario. To Gina, everyone else seemed more needy and deserving.

Clutching a tissue in one hand and holding a cigarette in the other, Gina cried, "No one is going to help me! I just have to deal with this situation on my own."

My heart went out to her. I spent the rest of our session coaching Gina on the power of self-compassion. By the end of our first meeting, Gina had agreed to ask for help four times. First, she would call the Employee Assistance Program (EAP) and make arrangements to meet with a psychologist or psychiatrist. Second, with the assistance of her coach and the EAP service, she would ask for time off. Third, she would ask her mother to care for her son for the next few days while she drove to the family cottage to rest. Finally, she was going to speak with her husband and ask him for his understanding and patience.

Gina deliberately chose to be self-compassionate, and in turn, it changed her life. She had tried doing it alone. Her physical and mental condition would no longer allow her to go on without assistance. She had little choice but to learn how to ask for help, and she did so by ignoring her fears and relying on the Applied Virtues.

What happened to Gina as a result of this deliberate choice to be self-compassionate? EAP jumped to her aid and convinced her boss that she was moving toward a breakdown. Immediately, she received permission to take four weeks off, which was eventually extended to eight. Gina's mother agreed, without hesitation, to care for her son for the weekend. Though Gina's husband didn't really understand, he accepted that she needed to be cared for.

Gina returned home, packed a bag and headed to the cabin in the woods. Once there, Gina slept for sixteen hours straight. When she awoke, she went for a walk, ate, and then slept another eight hours. Two days later, reassured by the help she had received and rested from the time alone, she rejoined her family. Within a week, she began to attend therapy and coaching sessions.

Three months later, Gina had completely changed her life for the better. Her relationship with her husband improved; they began to rely on each other more than they had before. She no longer worked thirty hours of overtime every week. Instead, possessed by the value of self-compassion, Gina became very protective of her time. Her energy returned, her excess weight disappeared, and her smoking habit was finally broken.

Gina experienced a serious breakdown. The moment I met her, I feared for her. Her desperation was palpable. She required a substantial shift in thinking and being. Her mind was focused on the wrong things and her body was no longer strong enough to enable any kind of personal change. She learned very quickly that the AV of self-compassion was the only way she could cry Mayday! She had to ask for help.

## STEP 3

# TAKE A LEAP

∎∎∎▬▬▬∎∎∎

*If you can't have faith in what is held up to you for faith,*
*you must find things to believe in yourself, for a life*
*without faith in something is too narrow a space to live.*
*George E. Woodberry*

Walter was in trouble. He had just had a difficult conversation with his boss. The big guy had made it perfectly clear that if Walter didn't stop micromanaging his teams, he'd never make it to the next level. Walter agreed to try, but he really didn't have a clue how to begin. Contributing to his nervousness was the fact that he had project kick-off meetings scheduled in Europe over the next couple of days. Literally overnight, Walter was expected to change how he worked with teams.

From a hotel room in Bonn, Germany, he called me for his regular coaching appointment. Walter explained that the first meeting was less than ten hours away and he had no idea what he should do. He knew he needed help.

I began by asking him how he had prepared for the

meeting. I could hear the pride in his voice as he described how he had planned everything down to the last detail.

I paused, and then inquired, "Walter, you've done so much already. What is it you need your team for?"

I love what happened next, Walter began to giggle. (I love it when tough guys giggle!) He admitted that he had taken care of pretty much everything and that there was little for the meeting participants to do.

Walter had overprepared because he had not wanted to appear disorganized or unprofessional. The riptide of shame was hard at work within him, convincing him that he had to be "in charge." Walter, under the delusions spouted by the fear of separation, was anxious that his career might be at an end if he didn't make substantial changes to his management style. Walter also resisted surrendering control of the project to anyone else. All three riptides were at work! To help Walter shift away from fear, we were going to have to rely on something more powerful: the applied virtue of faith.

"Right," I replied. "Then, I'm going to challenge you to take a leap of faith. I want you to rip up everything you've prepared for tomorrow. Right now—so I can hear you do it while I'm on the phone—I want to you to destroy the plans and schedules that you've already created. Go into the meeting tomorrow with a partial agenda. Write it on the board and then ask your team to generate other topics that need to be covered. Then I challenge you to ask your team to help you plan the rest of the project."

Walter was really laughing now. He felt the giddiness that sometimes accompanies a willingness to move into the unknown. After a bit more discussion, he agreed that this was the right course of action. By the end of the call, he agreed to this leap of faith.

## Step 3: Take A Leap, Practice Faith

You've completed Step 1 by taking a stab at naming your need and by vowing to remain open to other possible resolutions. And if you've applied the self-compassion required by Step 2, you have accepted that you are worthy of help. Now Step 3 challenges you to do what we all must do at some time in our lives: Take a leap of faith. If self-compassion *prepares* you, then the applied virtue of faith *supports* you as you send your mayday signal. As you read ahead, keep in mind the first anchoring principle: Emotion affects action and language. How we present ourselves and how we phrase our request is directly linked to the reciprocating power of emotion.

### Faith in What or Whom?

In whom or what does your faith lie? Faith can be a belief in something or someone greater than our selves, such as God, Buddha, the Goddess, or Allah. Others may put their faith in the wisdom of the Universe and the connectedness of all things. And still others direct their faith, not toward a supreme being, but toward the "natural order of things." Many simply accept, as a universal truth, that events or circumstances work out for the best. And a few believe in the law of percentages or playing the odds. (This last group likes to look at their past life and predict the future based on the odds: "The odds are that things will turn out all right.")

Some insist that faith in oneself is the best way to succeed in life. They caution that trusting others, organizations, or even the Divine, is a sure road to disappointment and failure. Trusting yourself, they advise, is the only way to go. Personally, I do not see how that is possible. I am the first to admit that I am imperfect and weak. Plus, my energy is easily drained. From experience, I know that when my personal energy reserves are low, my many weaknesses and flaws find their way to the surface. I am certainly not about to rely only on myself in such challenging times.

Some people believe in putting their trust in others. Again, I would advise vigilance here since, as a species, we don't have the best track record of follow-through and commitment. We mean well, but . . . even if you trust your helpmate one hundred percent, there will always be the possibility that things will not work out. Some person, thing, or event may stop him or her from fulfilling the commitment.

When it comes to asking for help and doing it in a clear and strong fashion, faith is what sees us through. Before we go further, spend a moment considering who or what you believe in.

## TRY THIS   YOUR BELIEF STATEMENT

Many religions and spiritual practices use credos or belief statements to reaffirm, inspire, and create a sense of community. Below is a sample.

♦ *I believe:* in a future that is filled with possibilities, some of which I cannot yet see. I believe in the power that arises when two or more people come together to solve any problem or to clarify any issue. I believe that the gifts and talents that I have been given are integral to my continued journey toward fulfillment of my life purpose.

♦ Your turn. Write your own belief statement.

*I believe:* _____

_____

_____

_____

_____

_____

## The Applied Virtue of Faith

"Faith is being sure of what we hope for and certain of what we do not see" (Hebrews 11:1). Whether you believe in God, possess a spiritual practice, or have none at all, faith requires you to let go of the tangible and reach for the unseen. It is a mystery, a trust beyond logic, that all will work out well. Faith can appear as a brief and fleeting absence of doubt or as an enduring internal confidence. It is called into action through prayer, meditative mantras, and that legendary leap of faith.

*The applied virtue of faith is a profound belief or understanding that we will be cared for, even when the outcome is doubtful or unclear.* This is exactly what we need as we make our requests for help: a belief that we will be all right. With this faith-based support, the oppressive and intimidating factors of asking for help diminish. And for some with deep faith, they disappear altogether.

Being cared for in our darkest hour does not mean that we will always have the help we desire, but that we will be provided with opportunities to learn and grow from every experience. Faith is confidence in a good end result. And if it doesn't seem to turn out as well as we'd hoped, it is simply because we do not yet see the conclusion.

Walter relied on faith to see him through his leadership challenge. He had no idea how the meeting would go the following day. He had no idea whether he would be able to connect with and lead his new team. He had no idea whether tearing up his agenda and plan was a good thing. All Walter really knew was that he would be taken care of, that it would turn out well. Based on this belief, Walter took his leap of faith toward the unknown.

Two days later, Walter called me from the airport. "It was incredible!" he exclaimed. "I walked in, went to the front of the room, took a deep breath and told the group that I needed their help in planning the project. I wrote up a few of the things I remembered from the agenda you had me destroy and I let them fill in the rest. The energy of the room changed immediately. It was like we were already working as a team, even though we had just met!"

Walter was unable to predict how it would all end, but he believed it would—somehow—work out. To make the shift from controlling boss to trusting leader, he would have to take a risk. His leap of faith unlocked his future and liberated him to move in a completely new direction.

With faith, all things are possible, even asking for and accepting help. Faith is the catalyst for miracles, or at least for very big and pleasant surprises. Faith is a step—sometimes tentative, sometimes audacious—into the unknown. When we take that step, we let go of the reins of life for just a little while. *The reassuring message of the AV of faith is that we are not alone; we are, and always have been, cared for.* It is this message that supports us as we send out our mayday calls.

## Hope and Faith

The AV of faith grows from the emotional seed of hope, a heartfelt wish for a positive future outcome. Hope assumes that our current conditions are unacceptable, and that something else would be preferable. A passive emotion, hope isn't vigorous enough to trigger an actionable response within us that leads to a more desirable future. "Hope is not a strategy," is a common refrain within political circles. This pithy statement simply reflects hope's less significant power and implies that something more is needed to effect change. As beautiful an emotion as hope is, it changes little. Unless and until we combine it with another powerful element, hope remains relatively ineffective.

# THE APPLIED VIRTUE MATRIX

| Applied Virtue | Definition | The Emotional Seed | Combined with | The Hidden Message |
|---|---|---|---|---|
| Faith | A deep belief that you will be cared for even if the outcome is unclear | Hope: an optimistic belief for the future | A leap of faith; surrender | You will be cared for; you are not alone |

Just as the rather passive emotion of sympathy can grow into life-altering compassion, hope can also lead to the un-conquerable AV of faith. There is, however, an important difference, in how this alchemy comes about. While the AVs of compassion and self-compassion require *action*, the AV of faith requires *inaction*. **To transform into faith, hope must be joined with a willingness to do nothing, to let others do for us, to surrender, to take a leap of faith.**

### Hope + A Leap of Faith = Faith

Think of the leap of faith as an actual and metaphorical intake of breath that happens just before you ask for aid. In our bod-ies, hearts, and minds, we hold that breath as we plunge into what comes next—whatever that is! For some, the leap of faith takes the form of a prayer like, "Please God. I leave my future in Your hands." For others, the leap shows up as "Well, here goes nothing!" Exactly. The "nothing" is what you are about to do.

## Acting from Faith: the Paradox

While self-compassion encourages us to *act* in our own best interests, faith is often about *not acting*. This is the paradox: In *not* doing something, we enable the applied virtue of faith to reach its full capacity. The *not doing* acts as a catalyst for the AV of faith to work its miracles. *Not doing* means a relinquishing of control, a letting go, so that someone or something else can manage the situation. As uncomfortable and frustrating as this is to our egos, there comes a point when we just have to surrender so faith can do its stuff.

Walter did what he could do—in fact, he did much more than was necessary. He prepared himself as though he were the only person on the team. Yet when it came down to it, Walter's final step was to not act. Instead, he let go of control and relied on his faith as he asked for the help he needed to make the project a success and to keep his career alive.

Regardless of your beliefs, you are probably very familiar with the concept of "a leap of faith." Throughout the centuries, the phrase has been used as shorthand to indicate that all avenues have been attempted; there isn't anything else to be done except let go. The phrase "leap of faith" is so commonly accepted that even the secular world acknowledges when it's time to "let it go" and "let the chips fall where they may." No matter who you are or what you believe, taking a leap of faith denotes philosophical surrender.

In modern-day Western cultures, doing nothing—letting go—is a hard sell. The very idea is hard to swallow for those who have been reared on a daily diet of control and self-sufficiency. When discussing this option, more than one person has stared at me and said, "Are you nuts?"

Surrender—stepping into the unknown—is often associated with white flags of failure. Acquiescing, giving up, or giving in do not result in the AV of faith. These are defeatist phrases that shift our emotional state toward feelings of powerlessness and despair. We do not want to feel that way, especially as we are about to ask for assistance. On the other hand, the phrases "letting go" and "relinquishing control" imply a mindful step toward a state of sincere acceptance.

When we do, we acknowledge our own limits and release ourselves to the power of faith.

♦ Refer back to the situation you described in Step 1: Name the Need.
Looking at your need, describe what it is you hope for.

♦ What is the personal leap of faith you must take in asking for help?

♦ Describe how you believe your faith will assist you in taking that
leap.

## Maggie's Story

What follows is a story of a woman of very strong faith. (As
you read her story, focus on the role that her faith played,
and not on her personal beliefs.)

Maggie was heavily involved in her local church and
when she found out that the congregation was organizing
a trip to Israel, she began plans to go along. She made sure
to attend all the meetings, update her passport and visa, and
even plan her wardrobe for the trip.

The only problem was that Maggie was broke. As a sub-
stitute teacher nearing retirement age, it was unlikely that she
would ever earn enough to go on such an expensive journey.
Every Sunday, her friends at church would surreptitiously
shake their heads in disbelief. "How could she possibly af-
ford it?" they would ask. Everyone knew Maggie was as poor
as a church mouse. What they didn't know was that Maggie
was a church mouse with deep faith.

Maggie was determined to go. She believed, without
question, that she was intended to see the Holy Land. Anytime a friend gently reminded her to "get real," Maggie
looked to her faith. She never expressed doubt, only amuse-
ment at her situation. I will admit that I was skeptical of her

plan myself. This was a pretty big dream Maggie had and I couldn't image that anyone was going to pay her way. Oh *me* of little faith!

Every day, Maggie had the chance to give up this fantasy. And every day, Maggie took a leap of faith. She continued to prepare for the journey, but her efforts were never focused on raising money. Instead, she relied on her faith to realign the world's energy so help could come to her. The act of letting go and surrendering to her faith removed Maggie from the trap of *doing*. With the applied virtue of faith, she was able to just *be* and allow God to *do* for her.

Five days before the scheduled departure, Maggie got a call from her pastor. An anonymous donor had offered to pay the way for two more parishioners to go to Israel! Would Maggie be interested in taking him up on this offer? Of course she would! Thankful, but not surprised, Maggie had known all along she would receive this gift.

The behaviors associated with faith are strong ones, the kind that move beyond the expected. With the AV of faith, we can make a dream real, break a streak of bad luck, and create a future that everyone else thought impossible.

## Faith and the Great Fears

Faith sends us reassuring messages that we are not alone and that we will be cared for. These messages become especially important as we are tempted by the same old warnings propagated by the riptides. With the AV of faith, these repetitive alarms lose their ability to frighten us.

Instead of running because we fear it, surrender must be embraced. This one critical component permits faith to work its magic. When we deliberately choose faith, we set in motion a series of powerful energies that make our fear of surrender inconsequential. The more often we let go, the more practical faith becomes. As with any other, the applied virtue of faith grows with deliberate and focused practice.

The fear of shame also weakens under the power of faith. What do we care how others perceive us when we know we are truly blessed? The opinions of those who do not understand cannot affect us. We will feel no shame about what we need because our faith reassures us that we will be just fine.

Finally, when we possess the AV of faith, we know we are cared for. As a direct result, the fear of separation loses its hold over us. Remember, this riptide lies to us, telling us that we are alone in this life. With faith, we see beyond the lie into the truth: We are not alone.

## The Effect of Faith on our Bodies and Minds

In 1522, Martin Luther wrote about faith, "It kills the Old Adam and makes us completely different people. It changes our hearts, our spirits, our thoughts and all our powers." These words can be easily said about any virtue. Just like the applied virtue of self-compassion, the AV of faith can't help but affect our minds and bodies. These changes become indispensable during our requests for help.

Sometimes, the transformation can be glorious. Have you ever watched as people experience the ecstasy that accompanies a faith based in religion or in God? They practically glow. Their faces shine with the confidence that they are loved. They feel a connection beyond this world. They become one with what they believe to be true. This is the effect of grace, the natural spiritual and physical side effect of faith.

Setting aside religious ecstasy, faith can alter our physical selves in different ways. Do you remember how our bodies lost some of their rigidity and became softer once we adopted self-compassion? Now, with faith, the body reflects a grounded energy. Anchored and supported, we become steady and secure. Even our energy slows its vibrations so our hands steady and our voices can become calm.

Fixed in our faith, breathing becomes easier and more regular. Our movements convey certainty, not doubt or worry. Instead of jerky or clumsy gestures, they become grace-full. We lift our faces up to the light—or at least straight ahead. Our eyes focus on the horizon before us as we anticipate a better, more positive future.

When we rid ourselves of the desire to control everything and rely on faith, the fear-based noise in our heads slows and drops in volume. Our thoughts become less frantic. Suddenly, there seems to be room to think. Our inner conversations shift. Instead of "I have to control this situation and handle it on my own," we say to ourselves, "I may not know how my request will be received, but I am willing to let go and see what happens."

If self-compassion gives us permission to send out a mayday call, faith strengthens and clarifies the signal. *With faith, your mayday cries will be delivered with clarity, quiet certitude, and strength.* Your language will reflect your belief, your certainty, and your confidence. Instead of wimpy requests like "I don't suppose you'd be willing to help me on this?" you will speak directly and without hesitation and say, "I need some help, can you help me?"

The deeper and more profound your beliefs, the more composed your words will be. You won't have to think about the words you use as you ask for the help you deserve. Instead, they will flow naturally and easily. With faith, you may be surprised at your own eloquence and persuasiveness!

Rather than relying on tears, we will speak with certainty that our need for help will be met. Rather than resorting to emotional blackmail, we will frame our requests with respect for ourselves and our helpmates. Rather than using coercion to get what we need, our words will be authentic and nonthreatening. With faith, we will be composed and fully self-possessed.

## Learning the AV of Faith

As children we hear stories of miracles, of situations that began with hopelessness somehow magically end with "And they all lived happily ever after." We internalize these and hope that some day, a miracle will come to us.

To truly learn the applied virtue of faith, another epiphany is required. Your awakening, like Walter's, probably won't be easy to come by. We acquire a deep understanding of faith when we risk something dear to us: our pride, our self-images, our egos. We must leave the ego behind as we take that running leap toward what we seek. This is not something others can teach us. We must experience faith for ourselves to truly understand its power.

Jane had her own personal epiphany with faith. She felt compelled to ask for help when, after a serious car accident, she found herself without transportation. In brainstorming a solution, Jane remembered that an ex-boyfriend often traveled extensively, sometimes for months at a time. Perhaps he wouldn't mind loaning her his car.

Jane had never before requested anything from this man. In their previous relationship, she took on the role of caregiver and supporter, not the other way around. Fiercely independent, Jane wasn't accustomed to relying on anyone, not her ex and not the Universe. She really had no idea whether he would agree to her request, but Jane hoped he would say yes.

Once Jane agreed that she deserved to ask for this favor, she purposely took her leap of faith. She told herself, "no matter what his response, everything is going to work out just fine." She resolved that if this old boyfriend rejected her, she'd find help from someone else.

After a few pleasantries, Jane spoke her request: "I totaled my car this week. I'm okay, but now I don't have a way to get to work. I remembered that you travel a lot. Would you be willing to loan me your car while you are gone?" Simple, straightforward. Jane found it surprisingly easy to ask for his help.

Jane laughed when she told us about how many times she dialed the phone before letting the call go through. Through it all, she experienced a great deal of doubt, and only a tiny little bit of faith that this was going to work in her favor. Eventually, she made the call a final time, and this time, she didn't hang up.

Even at its weakest, faith remains a powerful force. Thankfully, faith doesn't have to be as strong as steel rebar to work in our favor. In fact, as the metaphor reminds us, it can be as small as a mustard seed and still move mountains.

What really moved Jane to dial the number, stay on the line, and ask for what she needed was her belief that everything would work out. This was her leap of faith. Even though her faith could have been stronger, it supported her as she asked for this favor. Jane was thrilled when this man agreed to let her use his car for the entire month!

Not only did she receive the aid she needed at a difficult time, but Jane's relationship with her ex-boyfriend also changed. What had been an uncomfortable separation was now a renewed friendship. Another emotional connection that would not have happened had she stifled her request for help! This was a turning point for Jane. She began to ask for help more often, especially in her romantic relationships. Each time she made a request, she paid particular attention to her leaps of faith. She observed that they became easier over time. Now, she welcomes them and believes that all will be well—no matter what.

## Changing Perceptions with the AV of Faith

My college boyfriend Malcolm was a happy guy. I think that was why I was so attracted to him. I, on the other hand, was seriously pessimistic. One day, as I was lamenting a problem about a student loan, he hugged me and said, "Don't worry. It all works out." I stared at him in disbelief. How could he think that? How could he not see that good things only happen after much hard work and agony? It had never occurred to me that life works out just fine. I always thought we had to fiddle with it—make it happen ourselves. Though his grades might not have been as good as mine, Malcolm knew something about life that took me years to figure out.

Those who have faith, in a god or a lucky star, understand Malcolm's philosophy. When we work too hard at making something happen, when we try to force a conclusion, we waste our energy. These over-the-top attempts to control anything or anyone yank us from the river of life. Letting go, relying on our faith, can put us back in the flow. All Malcolm was really telling me was to stop worrying, slow down, and believe that it will all work out.

No wonder Malcolm was always happy! He knew, as did Maggie, that often the most effective action we can take is to not act, to let the world do what it needs to do. As long as we do what we can, the Universe can handle the rest.

## The Choice: The AV of Faith

Each applied virtue requires us to make a choice between the status quo, the way we currently conduct our lives, and a new path, one that is unfamiliar and uncomfortable. You can either choose to continue to "do" and to attempt to control, or to "not do," and let go. Activating the powers of the AV of faith requires that we select the virtuous path. This means we must purposefully relinquish control, ask for what we need, and experience what it's like to be cared for again.

**TRY THIS**   **GENERATING FAITH**

Here are some suggested activities to generating the applied virtue of faith:

◆ Sit quietly, observing your breath as you inhale and exhale. Allow yourself the luxury of three very deep breaths. Hold each inhalation for a moment, until you can feel your heartbeat, and then release it. Imagine yourself lying on a hill of green soft grass beneath a tree that stretches to the sky. The branches that sway in the breeze above you are dressed with leaves of a thousand colors. Each leaf represents a blessing that is a part of your life. Spend time inventorying each leaf and assigning to it all the things you value: great friendships, deep intimacies, regular security, financial support, etc. As you continue counting your blessings, remind yourself that you are not alone and that all is well.

◆ Sit quietly and envision yourself completing your request for help with grace and self-respect. Run this visualization through your head multiple times a day. With each new effort, deepen your confidence and self-assurance.

◆ Pray. Send out a prayer declaring your faith. Or pray for support and guidance as you make your mayday calls.

◆ Create a mantra that has meaning for you. It may be something as simple as your declaration of faith, or it may be a short quote that inspires you. Here's one by historian Stephen Ambrose: "The past is a source of knowledge, and the future is a source of hope. Love of the past implies faith in the future."

◆ Think back to a time of challenge and difficulty. Ask yourself how you came through it all. Where did you find the strength to get to the other side of the test? How did your faith serve you then? Once you have a clear idea, write down your experience as a story. Include all the characters involved as well as all the key events. Keep this story in a safe place so you can refer back to it during a time of need.

♦ Meditate on faith. Find a quiet spot, close your eyes, and breathe
  deeply. Focus your attention on your breath for the next few minutes. Anytime you notice your attention drifting from your breath,
  gently bring it back. When you are ready, allow your mind to consider faith: what it means, how it shows up in your life, and how it
  feels when you experience it. Again, if your mind shifts, return to
  your thoughts of faith. Don't just think about faith: imagine it, experience it, feel what it is like. When you are ready, shift your attention
  to your breathing. Then, slowly inhale deeply three times. On the
  third breath, open your eyes. Be sure to record in your journal any
  thoughts or revelations you experienced.

♦ Listen to your friends, co-workers, or family members when they
  tell you "everything will be fine." If you feel as though you want to
  dismiss their message of support, stop and choose to entertain the
  thought that perhaps they may be right. Hold on to that thought for
  as long as you can.

## Applying the AV of Faith to Asking for Help

Step 1 required you to define and name your need, as best you
can. Step 2 asked you to accept your worthiness to ask for what
you need. Now, Step 3 of the *Mayday!* process is all about letting go of your fears of surrender, separation, and shame and
embracing the power of the applied virtue of faith.

In this step, faith bolsters you as you make your request.
It takes your hopes, wishes, and dreams and blows life into
them so they can become realities. It provides support as you
take a leap of faith toward the unknown. Your leap is the catalyst that sets in motion the mysterious power of faith.

When you invite in the AV of faith your body will change.
Strong and centered, you will stand tall and your eyes will
connect with your helpmate's. As long as you possess faith—
and remember, quantity is not important as quality—you will
know that you are not alone, that all will be fine.

In the story that follows, you will see one person for

whom faith is an atrophied muscle. His very first opportunity to rely on faith wasn't exactly a calming experience. His leap of faith was a truly risky one. You will also read about a woman for whom faith, though not grounded in a religious tradition, was a living virtue.

## David's Story

Annette and David worked with each other at an international telecommunications company. David was a vice president who reported directly to the CEO. Annette reported to David. I coached both. It soon became clear that Annette and David were not getting along as well as they could. For the first month or so, a week didn't go by without one of them complaining to me about the other.

David's primary issue with Annette was that she just wouldn't accept any of the assistance he tried to give her. It seemed that the more time he spent with her, the more resentful she became. Of all his direct reports, Annette was the newest hire. He worried that her inexperience with the company might cause her difficulty, so David made it a point to give her more of his attention.

This drove Annette crazy. In her previous jobs, she had worked independently and, as a result, was confused by David's interest. She felt as though she was being set apart from her peers because David seemed to focus most of his energy on her. Over time, Annette came to view David as a micromanager. After a little more observation, I had to agree with her.

Thankfully, David was open to coaching. He soon realized his controlling behavior restricted both him and Annette. I suggested that he might want to select an upcoming assignment and allow Annette to run with it. "It doesn't have to be anything too risky," I cautioned.

A week later, I met with David. "I decided not to take a

little leap of faith as you suggested. Instead, I took a huge one," he said. David went on to explain that he was scheduled to present at a meeting of the senior leadership including the CEO. He decided to ask Annette to help him by taking it on herself. David called her into his office and told her that he was going to be unavailable for the meeting. He asked her to plan the presentation and then give it.

My breath was taken away by the size of the challenge, for both Annette and David. This would have been Annette's first time in front of senior management and David's first time letting go.

David continued. "Making the decision to ask Annette to take this on was rough. I wasn't sure I could do it and let her handle it without interfering. Once I made my decision, I was able to call her into my office and ask her to take on the assignment."

Clearly, David's mayday call was made easier because delegation is not only acceptable, but encouraged in most work environments—delegation is a suitable way to ask for assistance. Even a request for help from our bosses is euphemistically described as "delegating up." This made it a little easier for David to ask, but because he chose a high-risk situation, he still experienced stomach-churning, elevated levels of stress. He understood that he was giving up control in a very public venue. His fear of surrender was working overtime.

David finally relaxed when he heard that Annette had done a fabulous job. Everyone, including the CEO, had been quite impressed with her and her abilities.

## Annette's Story

Annette and I did not meet before her presentation to senior management, so I was curious to hear her perspective. Here is her story.

"David called me into his office last week. I thought he was going to go over the plan I had submitted for another project. It was something I was getting used to: his detailed reviews of my work product. Instead, he told me that he wanted me to take his place at the meeting." Annette was blown away by the assignment. She wasn't sure she understood his motives, but she didn't want to miss out on an opportunity to interact with upper management.

The night before the presentation, Annette realized what she was about to do. She had not bothered to involve David in her planning at all. Annette figured she must have unconsciously chosen not to involve David because of their previous difficulties. She was also caught in the riptide of the fear of surrender. The last thing she wanted to do was to ask David for his help because she thought she'd have to do everything his way.

Annette continued, "So, I just decided that I had to believe that everything was going to work out just fine. This opportunity wouldn't have dropped in my lap unless I was supposed to succeed with it. The meeting went great. I covered everything they needed and I was able to answer all of their questions. I even tossed in a joke that the CEO laughed at. Ever since then, things have been different between David and me—lighter, more fun. He doesn't crowd me anymore and I even ask for his help now and then."

Annette's faith came from a confidence in the natural order of life. She didn't appeal to a deity, she believed that life is good and that everything happens for a reason. Once she decided that everything would be fine, her faith quieted her fears and centered her body so she could field questions and connect with the company's leadership. She was poised enough to even crack a joke!

David also discovered how taking a leap of faith sets in motion a series of worthwhile lessons. He proved to himself that he didn't have to control every element of every situation. He also saw, firsthand, the practical nature of faith. He figured out that the best time to rely on faith was when all other options had been explored, or when life-changing lessons needed to be learned.

Taking those separate, but connected, leaps of faith returned David and Annette to the flow. Their relationship became easier and their work improved. Now when one of them is the least bit worried, the other smiles and says, "Have faith."

The moment to speak your request has come. It is now time to "make the ask," to show the world that you are a valued person, one worthy of help. It is time to show the world how to make a request for help with faith, clarity, and strength.

# STEP 4

# ASK!

■■■━━━■■■

Know how to ask. There is nothing more difficult
for some people, nor for others, easier.

*Baltasar Gracian*

The applied virtues of self-compassion and faith are powerful emotional states that turn asking for help into a declaration of self-love and self-care. For some of you, this may
be enough to get you out there asking for what you need.
Others, however, might require a review of the basics, or the
nuts and bolts, of transmitting effective mayday signals. This
chapter presents the who, when, where, and how of making
requests for help.

## Step 4: Ask!

There is no way around it, asking for help demands that we
actually *ask for help*. This time, *making the ask*, as salespeople
often say, is going to be much easier. Self-compassion encourages you to ask for the help you deserve. Faith supports

you as you make your mayday calls. Together, they relax and ground you physically and mentally. Your words and body reflect the belief that all will work out and that you are not alone. The suggestions that follow serve to create a supportive environment for your requests.

## Whom to Ask

Selecting just the right recipient of our mayday request is often a challenge. There is no one best answer, but you can use these guidelines as you consider your helpmate options.

### Check Out the Usual Suspects

Possible helpmates could include your spouse, significant other, family, friends, or co-workers. These are people with whom you already have some kind of relationship. If you've known each other for a while, then you've probably both experienced periods of abundance and lack. With familiarity, you may feel more comfortable anticipating their reactions to your call for help. Your first inclination may be to go with someone you know. However, there may come a time when you will think twice before you ask those who know and love you best.

Henry has confided that he only feels comfortable relying on his wife for help. He knows she feels obligated and sometimes this is a burden to her. At times, she chafes from being his only resource. Henry knows this is unfair. If you find yourself in a similar situation, challenge yourself to step beyond the safe and comfortable, to take a leap of faith toward another person.

Pause before you start making your requests for help. There is wisdom in stopping and slowing down. Find a quiet place to sit, breathe deeply, and give yourself a chance to quiet your body and your mind. This mental, physical, and emotional break serves to ground you. Resist any impulse to pick up the phone and make an immediate call for help, unless of course, your need is truly urgent.

Set your mind to the task at hand: expanding your list of helpmates. Use pen and paper; avoid typing your list on your computer. This slower, old-fashioned way of making a list decelerates your thinking, too. Then generate as many names of potential helpmates as you can. Follow the basic rule of brainstorming that dictates that no idea should ever be rejected this early in the process. That means you can put down names of people who may say no. Now is not the time to cross off possibilities before your list even gets started.

### Be Creative; Look Beyond the Obvious

Make it a point to add new names to your list. You may not even know the people you add. This new addition may be a friend of a friend. Perhaps you know them only by reputation. Have fun with your list. I usually add Richard Branson's name because he's an entrepreneur and philanthropist whom I admire. In my imagination, I fancy that he would certainly be open to requests like mine. Silly, of course. I've never met Sir Richard, but just seeing his name on the list lightens my mood. And that's always a good thing in a time of need.

Spend time pondering the six degrees of separation. The theory goes that everyone in the world can be reached through a series of fewer than six different connections. Apply this theory to your life. For example, if you seek help with your physical well-being, consider talking to a yoga instructor or to someone who strikes you as being fit and healthy. She may be able to lead you to a healer or physician she values greatly. Or if you need help balancing work and home, consider talking to the neighbor down the street who always seems to have plenty of time for his kids. He might not be able to help you directly, but maybe he can suggest someone who can.

### Assume Nothing

Remember, during this time of need, your fears are lying like dogs. Your ego-mind is working overtime to get your attention and force you to scratch off names as soon as you add them to the list. Don't do it. That insidious little voice wants you to believe that everyone else is too busy to help. Or that your long shots are just too long (like Richard Branson). Don't listen to it. The point of this activity is two-fold. First, to produce a list that can also be used in the future, and second, to reinforce that you are blessed with a strong network of those willing and able to help you.

---

**TRY THIS**   **CREATE A HELPMATE LIST**

Use the following template to create a list of potential helpmates. Update it periodically, depending on your need.

Name                              Contact Information

1. _____    _____

2. _____    _____

3. _____    _____

4. _____    _____

5. _____    _____

6. _____    _____

7. _____    _____

### Be Willing to Be Surprised

You might find that as you make your list, serendipity drops by for a visit. You might get a surprise phone call from someone who is the ideal person to help you, or you might find the perfect helper from reading the newspaper. Once you are ready to ask for help, then everything starts to align in your favor. Some refer to this phenomenon of alignment as the Great Shopping Mall in the Sky. The philosophy goes like this: Many angels in heaven are waiting for us to decide what it is we need and want. They stand there in their white gowns and wings holding onto those old-fashioned order pads (the kind that department store sales associates used to use before everything became automated). As soon as we know what we need and send off our prayers, they jump into action. They scribble our orders down on those pads and then send them off to be fulfilled. Our only obligation is to remain vigilant and open to whom and what shows up next.

### Sleep on It

Once your list is made, and if time allows, put it away. After a day or so, go back to the list. Give yourself time for the list to speak to you. Trust your intuition. It may move you to select the name you resist the most, or the one you know the least. Once you've made your choice, elicit the AV of faith. Your faith will reassure you that you've made the best choice possible.

### Create a Support Team

A proactive step that you can take well before you ever need to send out a mayday call is to create a support team of your own. Many of us rely heavily on family and co-workers, but most of these people were not deliberately chosen by you to be in your life. As loving as they may be, these accidental affiliations may not be the best helpmates for you. As in all things, mindful choice is preferred. Rather than choosing the default options—husband, wife, or friend—build a deliberate and functioning support team of select individuals. Your support team might consist of:

- ◆ One person who will commiserate with you and then cheer you up.

- ◆ One person who will challenge your perceptions and beliefs.

- ◆ One person who is unlike you in many aspects such as culture, personal history, and areas of interest.

- ◆ One person to act as your scout: someone who has been where you are and is willing to share his or her experiences with you.

- ◆ One person with a wicked sense of humor who will get you to laugh.

If you have a team like this already, you may be able to find help quickly and with very little angst. If not, the best time to establish such a team is when you are feeling strong and confident.

## When to Ask

There are no hard and fast rules for when to send out your mayday signals. You might want to use these guidelines as you prepare to ask.

### Avoid the Rush

It is tempting to believe that many of our pressing needs must be resolved immediately. This isn't always the case. Ask yourself if your need is pressing; if there is a time element that needs to be addressed. We often confuse urgency with importance. Some needs are important, but not urgent. You might feel the need to buy groceries (an important task), but if your child calls from the hospital (an urgent task) the groceries will wait. Conversely, some needs are urgent, but not necessarily important. Your teenage daughter may insist that she needs to be driven immediately to the local skateboarding park. She may feel it is urgent to hang out with her friends. You know, however, that this is not an important request, especially if homework is yet to be completed.

Ask yourself, "Does this need have to be met now?" and "How important is it for this need to be fulfilled?" The answers to these questions can help you avoid delivering your request in a rushed or panicked manner.

Sandy, a temporary office worker, didn't always have enough work to enable her to pay her rent. She dreaded asking anyone for help, but there were times when it just couldn't be avoided. Her usual practice was to wait until her rent was overdue and then make a call to Randi, her older sister. Randi didn't mind loaning the money, but what aggravated her was that Sandy always waited until the last moment. What was an important need became an urgent one. This meant that Randi felt forced to take time away from work to go to the bank to wire the money. She also incurred additional charges for the transfer. "Why can't Sandy let me know a week before the rent is due? Why does she always ask me at the last minute?" Randi asked.

If you anticipate that you'll need help in the near future, then speak to your helpmate as early as possible. Avoid waiting until your important need becomes pressing. Advance notice is almost always welcome. If it turns out you don't need help after all, your helpmate will be pleased. If you do need it, she will appreciate the heads up.

## Banker's Hours

Think about what time it is when you ask for help. Your fear may attempt to convince you that the call must be made immediately—no matter what time it is. Like the other lies told by your fear, this one isn't true. Most of our mayday requests can be sent out during normal business hours, or at the very least, during the day. Avoid dinnertime and late evening as much as you can.

If you need help from someone at work, find a time when schedules are lighter or even clear. Use a lull in the craziness to make your request.

## Ask Early, Ask Often

In Chicago, we have a saying that started in the old days of the political machines, "Vote early and vote often." This tongue-in-cheek admonition can apply to asking for help, too.

Consider the possibility that you may have to ask more than one person for assistance. If after getting a negative response to your first request, slow yourself down again. Avoid rushing in and asking someone else right away. Regroup. You might feel a little wounded at the rejection, so spend a moment to stir up a little more compassion for yourself. Then, re-establish your link to faith. Be sure these applied virtues are firmly in place before you ask the next person on your list for help.

## Listen to Your Intuition

Your intuition will likely tell you when it's "a good time" to ask. Pay attention to what's happening with your helpmate. Notice if he is under stress or if it's a particularly difficult day. Do your best to move beyond your own fear to empathize with the person who might actually be able to help you out.

## Where to Ask

### In Person

Successful mayday calls require full and honest conversations—instantaneous and reflexive give-and-take of statements, questions, and answers. If at all possible, make your request in person. The one-on-one conversation has multiple benefits. First, you'll be better able to judge the openness and empathy of your potential helpmate. You'll be able to see for yourself if she's having a bad day or if she is suffering under the weight of her own issues. Second, your body communicates more than your voice and speech does. A centered physical presence, with excellent posture and a confident demeanor, has the best chance of making your request work. Finally, you'll be able to care for your relationship, reacting immediately to any energetic or emotional shifts that might occur. If, for example, your helpmate becomes confused, you'll have a chance to quickly resolve any confusion.

If you must present your request via email or letter, be sure to take it slowly. Just as if you were meeting with your potential helper in person, spend a moment or two to collect your thoughts and to generate self-compassion and faith. As soon as you do, your words are more likely to flow. Read the letter over carefully before you hit the *Send* button or drop it in the mailbox. Again, if time allows, pause and breathe. Leave the draft on your computer and sleep on it. The next day, take a look at it again with fresh eyes.

### In Private

If you are at work, find an empty office or conference room to make your request. Avoid asking for what you need in the corridors or cafeteria. Creating a space of privacy accomplishes two things. First, it demonstrates the seriousness of your request. Second, it frees your potential helpmate to respond candidly. You will both be less concerned about prying eyes or big ears if the two of you speak alone. If you want to make a personal request of a friend or family member, invite him over to your home for a private chat, but only if it is convenient and comfortable for him. Otherwise, make your request on his home turf. Do what you can to make your helper feel comfortable.

### Limit Distractions

Put away the Blackberries and turn off the phones. Shut the office door or tell your assistant to hold all calls. Silence your email chirps. If you are at home, be sure the kids are occupied and the dog is taken care of. Let the answering machine get your calls. Your mayday signal will be more easily received if there are no interfering distractions. Focus all your attention on this new conversation.

## How to Ask

As long as you possess the grace born from the applied virtues of self-compassion and faith, the "how" of your request becomes less of an issue. Remember that the applied virtues, just like emotions, affect the actions we take and the words we speak. If you possess self-compassion and faith, your words and actions will convey those powerful states of being. Here are some additional guidelines to consider:

### Remain Open

Remember that your emotional state has likely blinded you to the possibilities that exist. It is mentally and emotionally challenging for you to know the best way to meet your need as long as you are affected by that need. Even though you cannot fully see, others can. Remain open.

### Brainstorm

Ask your helpmate to brainstorm solutions with you. If you have a deliberate and functional support system already in place, then you can ask your team to come up with creative solutions with you. If not, go to someone you know and respect for their wisdom. Briefly, the rules of brainstorming are:

♦ All ideas are equally welcome and valid. There are no dumb ideas.

♦ Avoid criticizing the ideas of others.

♦ Build on everyone's ideas.

♦ Go for quantity over quality. The idea is to generate the most creative, not necessarily the most practical ideas.

### Ask Questions

If you've got faith the size of a mustard seed and find yourself a little nervous, you might want to tuck away a few standard questions that will help get your conversation going. Here are some good ones:

♦ Would you be willing to help me with something? Is now a good time?

♦ I've got something I'm trying to resolve, can you give me a hand?

♦ (Using humor) I'm desperate, can you help me please? (Advisable only if you have an established relationship with your potential helpmate).

♦ I'm stuck and I can't see clearly how to resolve this.
Would you be willing to help me come up with a few
ideas?

And if they are not able to help, ask:

♦ Can you suggest someone else who might be able to
help?

♦ Do you know anyone who has had a similar situation?
Do you know how they resolved it?

## Getting Clear on Next Steps

After you have gone through so much to prepare your mayday signals, it would be a shame if your needs still went unanswered because of an unclear agreement on what happens
next. It would be equally or even more disappointing if your
relationship suffered because of communication problems.
So much of our personal anguish comes about when prom-
ises are left unfulfilled. Ask yourself the following questions
to make sure you avoid these kinds of issues:

### What Is the Objective?

It's important for both of you to understand the goal you are
working toward. Use the results of your gap analysis to explain the situation. Unless you are willing and able to laugh
it off if a different goal is achieved, then be sure to talk this
through carefully.

### What Are the Next Steps?

Get as detailed as you can in identifying key activities or
steps. It's not okay to micromanage your helpmate, but it is

permissible to get an idea of the major steps to be taken. You may never know how your need is met. That just means that you really have to let go of the riptide fear of surrender. Usually, you do have an idea of what's involved. If so, then offer to work up a plan or suggest key activities that will need to be completed. Your helpmate will appreciate the clarity.

### When Will the Help Be Rendered?

If you have a set timeline or deadline that has to be met, be sure to inform your helpmate. She may be willing to help, but she may not be able to do it in your timeframe. You may have to negotiate a date that works for both of you. Again, let go of your fear of surrender. If no deadline looms, then suggest a schedule that works for both of you.

### Is This a One-Person Job or Will Your Helpmate Enlist Others to Help?

Some needs are sensitive and should be kept private. If you do not want others to know that you are being helped, be sure you inform your helpmate that you'd like to keep this hush-hush. If privacy isn't an issue, ask your helper if she might know of someone else who can contribute to the process.

### Does Quality Matter?

If a task has to be finished with a certain level of quality, say an application has to be fully and accurately completed, then be specific about those requirements. More than likely, your helpmate wants to assist in the best way possible, so be sure to be as specific with these details as you can. Both of you would feel badly if your helpmate thought he had done a great job when, in actuality, he hadn't.

### What Is Your Role?

Wouldn't it be nice if our helpmates just went off and fixed our problems without us? Nice, but unlikely. It would also be irresponsible for us to expect that. Offer whatever you can to make sure that you are both successful. Be available to provide additional assistance, if necessary.

### What Might Get in the Way of Getting the Task Done?

An uncomfortable question, to be sure, but one that still can be asked. If you believe your helper might have difficulty keeping her promise to you, then discuss it in advance. Avoid waiting until the problem becomes too big for both of you to handle.

### How Will You Know When the Promise of Help Has Been Fulfilled?

Your help may arrive and you may never even know it. Ask your helper to inform you when he's kept his promise.

## Letting Go—Again

Occasionally I find that it's still possible for my fears to change my mind. There are times, after I've spoken the words and while the sound of my voice is still floating in the air, that I feel the urge to take it all back. Perhaps my faith wasn't as strong as I would have liked, or maybe I lost sight of my blessings. Whatever the reason, I sometimes feel the impulse to add, "Oh never mind. I'm sure I can handle this by myself." Or just as bad, "Oh forget it. I know how busy you are. Don't worry about me."

In these brief moments, when doubt creeps in, I have to relocate my faith and let go—again. I've discovered a few simple ways to regenerate faith that may prove useful to you as well.

## TRY THIS   THE AGREEMENT

As you talk over the implementation of your request for help, use the following form to guide your discussions. Or use it to help you collect your thoughts before you make your mayday call.

| Objective: | Deadline or Timeframe: |
|---|---|
| Key Steps: | Key People: |
| 1 _____ | 1 _____ |
| 2 _____ | 2 _____ |
| 3 _____ | 3 _____ |
| Quality Requirements: | My Role: |
| 1 _____ | |
| 2 _____ | |
| 3 _____ | |
| Signs of Completion: | Possible Interference: |
| 1 _____ | 1 _____ |
| 2 _____ | 2 _____ |
| 3 _____ | 3 _____ |

First, I breathe. That simple intake of oxygen has become my best reward. There are times I feel as though I'm holding my breath—both metaphorically and physically—when I ask for help. Just after I take my leap of faith, I allow myself a good, deep, chest full of free air. This simple reconnection to the abundance of life—there's always plenty of air—helps me slip right back into faith.

Next, I make a simple gesture or small movement. Nothing too distracting, but enough to ground me and keep me centered. If I'm standing during my request, I double-check to make sure my feet are securely grounded, which might require me to shift a little in my shoes. If I'm seated, I can always do the same thing. I push my feet into the floor, imagining that I am rooted to the Earth. This steadies me and prevents me from snatching back my request.

Talismans can also be helpful when people articulate their mayday cries. Lucky stones or old pennies, talismans seem to provide their owners with a grounded strength. I know one woman who has a lucky pearl bracelet. As long as she wears that, she remains strong and resolute. These easy ideas can prevent us from succumbing to fear at the last moment.

## Jack's Story

Jack was a sixteen-year-old high-school student with middling grades. A bright kid, he was diagnosed with dyslexia when he was twelve. The last four years had been a challenge for him. He had spent a great deal of time hiding, from pretty much everyone, the fact that he had a learning disability. He couldn't shake the feeling that his tendency to invert numbers and letters was going to keep him out of college. "How am I ever going to take the SAT if I can't read it properly?" he wondered.

Jack was afraid to send out a mayday call; the riptides of fear *really* had him. He thought, for sure, word would leak out to his friends that he needed special "help." I could see that his fear of shame convinced him he'd never be able to live it down. Afraid to be seen as "special" or different from anyone else, Jack was also paying too much attention to the lies spread by the fear of separation. What he feared most was to surrender to the disability. A determined kid, he worked like crazy to make sure that his dyslexia didn't get in his way to get what he wanted: a college education. "I can't be the only kid who's gone through this before. Somebody has got to help me," he reasoned.

Jack needed help and he had an idea who might be a good person to ask: Mrs. Paulson. Mrs. P taught art appreciation in addition to drawing and painting. Jack seemed to do well in her classes, so he felt a bit more comfortable talking to her.

Nervous, but working hard to hide it, Jack asked Mrs. P

on Monday if she'd save a few minutes after class on Wednesday to talk to him. She agreed. Jack could tell she was pretty curious, but she didn't ask why.

In preparation for their talk, I suggested that Jack write down a few notes for himself. Capturing his thoughts on paper would force him to think about how he wanted to present himself. I also encouraged him to decide how he wanted to feel when he went in to talk with his teacher. Did he want to appear confident or nervous? Optimistic or anxious? "Oh I want to be confident all right. I just don't want her talking to anyone else about my problem," he replied.

Jack took a first good step by asking for an appointment, rather than just trying to get his teacher's attention during class. This meant he was also able to limit the chance that anyone would overhear their conversation. Jack had also selected Wednesday because his last period was phys ed. He figured he could burn off a little of his nervous energy by running or lifting weight before heading to the art room. Just in case nerves got the better of him, Jack decided to memorize his opening line.

Wednesday arrived. Once the classroom cleared, Jack walked up to his trusted teacher and sat in the chair adjacent to her desk. He pulled out his few notes and took a deep breath. Then he looked her in the eye and said, "I'm not sure what to do. I really want to go to college, but my grades aren't that great." Smiling, Mrs. Paulson interrupted, "How can I help?"

Jack was caught off guard, just a little. He didn't expect an interruption when he practiced his opening. So, he looked down at his handwriting for a moment to gather his thoughts. "I haven't told many people, but I have dyslexia." He looked up at Mrs. P just to see her reaction. There wasn't one, so Jack moved on to his leap of faith, "If I'm going to get into college, I'm going to need some help. I just don't have any idea where to start. I thought maybe you could help me."

His teacher thought a moment and asked, "Well, this is an unusual request for an art teacher, but sure, I'll be happy to help."

Relief washed over Jack. For the first time since he had decided to ask for help, his shoulders relaxed. He realized that asking for what he needed didn't have to be so hard after all.

Suddenly, it became a whole lot easier. The questions just poured out him. "What do you think I need to do? Do you really think we can fix it so I can take the SAT?" Jack asked her when she thought she'd be able to get back to him with some answers. He also inquired about her schedule. Did she really have the time to help him? Surprised by his concern for her, Mrs. P smiled. "If you need the help, Jack, I'll make time. Don't worry." Together, they brainstormed next steps and how they might go about preparing Jack to take the test.

After they talked a while, Jack asked the hardest question of all, "Can we keep this quiet? I don't really want anyone to know." Mrs. P understood his concerns and told him that she'd keep it as quiet as possible, but that she might have to talk to the counseling office about his request. Reluctantly, Jack decided that was okay just as long as none of his friends found out.

Jack had done a wonderful job at asking for help. He had prepared himself. He had sought the one person whom he trusted most. He made his request in a private setting in a room where his helpmate felt most comfortable and where he was sure he would have Mrs. P's undivided attention. By asking on Monday to talk on Wednesday, he had even given himself more time to calm down. Expressing sincere concern for her and her needs, he engendered even more empathy within Mrs. P. Together they decided on what was to happen next.

Let's check where we've come so far.

We've spent time in serious consideration of our need, creating a first guess at how to meet the need. We've also learned how to conjure self-compassion and faith. The applied virtue of self-compassion reaffirms that we are worthy and deserving of the help we seek.

Our mayday signal been sent or spoken. How we present ourselves and how we phrase our request is directly linked to the reciprocating power of emotion. Possessing—and being possessed by—the applied virtue of faith, we reflect the confidence we feel. Fear cannot muddy the signal. Instead, we deliver our requests for help with certitude that we will be helped.

In that space of time between when you ask for what you need and the response from your helpmate, there is time to generate one more applied virtue: gratitude.

# BE GRATEFUL

∎▮▮━━━▮▮▮

> Gratitude is not only the greatest of all virtues,
> but the parent of all the others.
> *Cicero*

Gratitude is the third applied virtue that transforms us. Even more than the other two virtues of self-compassion and faith, gratitude bolsters us as we make our mayday calls. It braces and supports both self-compassion and faith. By seeing how we've already been blessed, it's easier to believe we will be blessed again. With gratitude in our hearts, all applied virtues come to us more naturally. Cicero was right, gratitude "is the parent of all others."

## Step 5: Be Grateful, Practice Gratitude

While self-compassion compels us to ask for the help we need, and faith centers us as we make our request, gratitude allows us to hear the response with an open heart. We naturally feel grateful hearing a response of yes, but can we feel the same way if the dreaded no is delivered instead? *This, then, is the power of gratitude: the prospect of hearing "no" causes us no fear. With gratitude, we will truly be grateful even if a request isn't fulfilled.*

## Distractions

Even with all that gratitude does for us, we often forget to be grateful. We forget because we remain focused on the wrong things.

It becomes all too easy, especially when we are at our weakest, to notice only what is missing, what doesn't yet exist, or what existed but is no longer present. Our fears nag at us, warning that we risk too much when we ask for help. They insist, "You might lose what little you do have of love, safety, and self-respect."

We spend so much of our energy making sure we have all we could ever want—and more. We've created a habit out of acquisition. If we aren't out at the shopping malls, then we're paging through catalogs or ordering items online. Shopping isn't a purely American pasttime any more. It's practically the national sport of Singapore and Japan. Yet are we any more grateful for what we have? Does having more make us feel gratitude? The opposite appears to be true: Our constant buying habits de-value what we already possess.

This attention to what's missing also affects not just our purchases but our personal relationships too. The divorce rate, for example, is as high as it has ever been. Couples complain about what's missing in their marriage rather than celebrating what is already there. I wonder if some of these relationships really need to be "fixed." What if each spouse appreciated, with sincerity and love, the person sleeping on the other side of the bed?

We also have an economy that is based on what's missing. The central tenet of capitalism is the law of supply and demand. Value is placed on those items that are scarce. This means that those things we have plenty of are seen as less important or less valuable.

At work, we direct our impressive analytical skills to the problems at hand. Not meeting our goals? Let's analyze what's wrong. An employee giving us trouble? Let's see what mistakes have been made in developing him. Rarely do we attend to the abundant talents and skills that keep our businesses going. Instead we learn to analyze and criticize, and we promote those who can identify what's wrong fastest and fix it quickest.

What I've been describing is the philosophy of scarcity. This cockeyed focus on lack, on what's missing, and on self-protection comes from a central belief that resources are scarce. We reason that if a thing is rare, then there may not be enough for us! Victoria Castle writes in *The Trance of Scarcity* of how we even feel *we* are "not enough." Not good enough, smart enough, or talented enough to get what we want. Castle explains that we don't even know we're addicted to this idea of "not enough"—we're caught in a trance.

The work world is starting to recognize the opposite philosophy, the presence of abundance. Instead of seeing what is missing, perhaps we need to see what is already present. A fascinating change management theory developed by Dr. David Cooperrider of Case Western University is called Appreciative Inquiry (AI). Cooperrider's approach relies on individual and group strengths to create organizational change. AI capitalizes on what we already do well. It is the antithesis of traditional change management methods that zero in on the identification and elimination of issues (read problems). Instead, AI incorporates a deliberate examination of success and explores ways to create more of it.

Introducing the concept of AI to an individual or group

elicits a predictable response, "How can AI possibly work? If we only spend time on what we do right, when do we fix the problem?" That's just the point. The skills of critique and analysis are so ingrained in our business psyches that we automatically seek out what's wrong and what's missing. It doesn't occur to most of us to begin by looking at our assets.

**TRY THIS    SCARCITY-BASED DISTRACTIONS**

What distracts you from seeing abundance in your own life? Focusing on what's missing increases stress, which is not something we need more of when asking for help. Spend time getting clear on your personal distractions.

♦ Spend one day recording in your notebook or journal those times when you found yourself focusing on the negative. Review your notes at the end of the day and see if there were times when you could have chosen to see a situation, event, or interaction differently. Then spend the next day focusing only on the positive. Now that your awareness has been piqued, look for more opportunities to acknowledge and celebrate the abundance around you.

♦ Observe how others see life. Do they talk and act from a starting point of scarcity? Listen to their words, as they reflect what is felt inside. Watch their behaviors, since these also reflect their hidden beliefs.

♦ Instead of skipping over or ignoring television commercials, watch them all for just one evening. See how many messages of scarcity you can identify. What do the advertisers imply you will lose if you don't buy their products? What do they imply will happen if you do? Which of your fears do their products *protect* you from?

What if, instead of focusing our attention on what's missing or wrong, we turned our gaze toward the blessings we already possess? What if we broke the addiction of "not enough?" What if we deliberately and with serious consideration looked at life the way it was meant to be seen—as full of abundance? What if, instead, we created new practices based on mindful appreciation?

## The Applied Virtue of Gratitude

That's where gratitude begins, of course—with appreciation. Defined by *Encarta World English Dictionary* as a "full understanding of the meaning and importance of something," appreciation is a simple, uncomplicated emotion. If sympathy is the seed that can blossom into self-compassion, and hope is the spark that can inspire our faith, then appreciation is the starting point for the applied virtue of gratitude. Like sympathy and hope, appreciation results in minor actions, not much more than a nod of the head or a spoken thank-you. Appreciation is a wonderful feeling, but it isn't enough to support us as we reach out from our own vulnerability and ask for the help we deserve.

We know that each of the seed emotions (sympathy, hope, and appreciation) must be paired with another element to take us to the level of applied virtue. Sympathy needs action, hope needs a leap of faith. Appreciation requires mindfulness. Mindfulness transforms simple appreciation into the life-changing virtue of gratitude.

### Appreciation + Mindfulness = Gratitude

If we can break the trance that scarcity holds over us, if we can remember to pay attention to the abundance that already exists, then gratitude has a chance to grow.

Do you remember Gina? Overwhelmed by the demands of motherhood and an unemployed husband, Gina required substantial help to get her life back in order. All she could see in front of her was her long list of obligations and worries. By focusing on all that was wrong, Gina inadvertently invited more of it into her life. Gina didn't realize that continuing to concentrate on the unhappiness in her life only brought her more unhappiness. As unpleasant as it might be, our bodies and psyches become accustomed to this state, making personal change even more difficult.

Caught in perpetual unhappiness, Gina resisted the idea of asking anyone for help. Even though my arguments about self-compassion and faith were intriguing to her, they weren't enough to shift her out of her miserable state. Trying to facilitate change on a grand or small scale doesn't work when one only appeals to the intellect. I couldn't talk Gina into crying Mayday! I gave up trying; I let her convince herself.

I directed Gina to go to the whiteboard and to write out, in large bold letters, as many of her life's blessings she could think of. Gina wrote a name at the very top of her list. I asked if it was her husband's. Gina turned to me and smiled for the first time that day, "No, it's my son." Buoyed by the thought of her little boy, Gina went to work creating a long list of blessings that soon covered the entire whiteboard.

To truly experience the AV of gratitude, we must remain aware of all that is important and of value. Deliberate awareness helps us attract a new energy, the grateful kind. Drowning in her own pain, Gina had forgotten all about her personal treasures. She desperately needed to become mindful of a different reality: how blessed she really was. Immediately, her overall perspective began to change. The applied virtue of gratitude cleared her mind of fear-based static and made possible a series of mayday calls.

Lost in fear and weak with exhaustion, we lose track of reality. Fear enjoys this because it now has a fertile environment in which to grow. Once rooted, it presents a reality where we are doomed to separation, shame, and surrender. Don't believe it; *fear lies to us about what is real.* The last thing fear wants us to discover is that our existence is amazingly different. Fear doesn't want us to remember the love we already have, the safety and security we already possess, and the health and well-being that supports our life. **Contrary to what**

# THE APPLIED VIRTUE MATRIX

| Applied Virtue | Definition | The Emotional Seed | Combined with | The Hidden Message |
|---|---|---|---|---|
| Gratitude | A profound appreciation for life's blessings | Appreciation: an understanding of the importance or value of something | Mindfulness | You are blessed! |

*the ego wants us to believe, gratitude's message is based in truth: We are blessed. This is the hidden message that our fear doesn't want us to discover.*

Simply by standing and writing in large colorful letters, Gina's focus swung from scarcity to abundance. She stopped looking at was missing and began noticing and celebrating what was in front of her all along. The AV of gratitude took hold of Gina. In that very moment, I watched as she breathed the first breath of her new life.

I know what Gina felt that day. We've all been in that dark emotional alley, waiting for the worst to happen when suddenly a light comes on and drives the shadows away. Gratitude is not just a little light, but a beacon that displays, in complete clarity, all the gifts of love and life that have been given to you. While your fears insist on pointing out what you might not have, gratitude proclaims the hidden and very real truth that you are blessed.

## TRY THIS    YOUR GRATITUDE LIST

What are you grateful for? Use the suggestions below to help you create your list.

♦ Within my relationships, I am grateful for_____

♦ Within my work environment, I am grateful for_____

- ◆ Within my social circle, I am grateful for_____

- ◆ Within my home, I am grateful for_____

- ◆ Within my hobbies and interests, I am grateful for_____

_____

- ◆ Within my long list of talents, I am grateful for_____

_____

## Gratitude's Effect on Our Bodies and Minds

Grateful people smile, not just with their mouths, but with their eyes, too. Their faces radiate a warmth that comes from within. It's as though they have a secret that no one else knows. Grateful people know they are lucky. They perceive that not only do they have all that they need, but they have more than most.

When the AV of gratitude takes hold of us, we experience an emotional and physical lightness, perhaps because we feel less encumbered by worries and cares. These concerns no longer have the power to weigh us down. With gratitude, our backs remain unbowed. If we bend at all, it is only to offer a silent word or two of thanksgiving.

Our gestures are careful when we are possessed by gratitude. Those who appreciate the value of their gifts always treat them with tenderness. If we ask to borrow anything—money, a car, a vacuum—then we will treat it respectfully, making sure that it is returned safely. If we require a personal favor, we will protect the generosity of our friends.

Our words change when we believe that our needs will be met. Remember how faith helps us speak our appeals plainly and without confusion? When gratitude is added to the mix, each word spoken will be delivered with appreciation. It is difficult to describe, but gratitude-soaked sentences almost seem, well, happy. Gratitude helps us to not care about what's missing. Instead of complaining, my mind and voice will say, "I am lucky," and "I am blessed."

Gratitude alters our personal frequencies. We vibrate at a different level, knowing that we are blessed. There is a frisson, a smooth electricity, that moves through our bodies. Our physical selves and language can't help but reflect the happiness born of a deep appreciation of good fortune.

## Acting from Gratitude

Each applied virtue directly affects our actions and language. If we possess self-compassion and faith, our behaviors and words will be compassionate and faithful. In the same way, the emotion of appreciation and the AV of gratitude have their own associated behaviors. Both move us to make offerings of thanks. With the seed emotion of appreciation, we show our thankfulness in small ways such as a verbal thank-you or a written note. The AV of gratitude, on the other hand, causes us to not just *say* thanks, but to *give* thanks.

Deliberate and profound appreciation—gratitude—is almost too big a feeling to keep in. It must be given in return. When I experience gratitude, I feel as though my heart is simultaneously heavy with love and light with joy. As I meditate on this virtue, I imagine myself standing with my arms raised in a meadow filled with flowers. The sun peeks in and out between the clouds. There is a slight breeze. In my mind's eye I see thousands of flowers springing from my chest. Blooms of all colors tumble out of me, covering the ground and mixing in with those that have already taken root. This image, for me, is one of offering, of giving thanks. I see it as a reciprocation of blessings, a giving back for all that I have received. (I've found it more than serendipitous that many of the well-known quotes on gratitude apply the metaphor of flowers. For example, from Henry Ward Beecher, "Gratitude is the fairest blossom which springs from the soul." How perfect! Gratitude is the natural beauty that cannot be contained—it must be released.)

When gratitude takes hold of our souls, we become naturally effusive. Yet, even as we burst with thanks, we know that our words will fail to convey the depth of our thankfulness. Perhaps that's why we use phrases like, "thanks a million" or "thanks a bunch." When the AV of gratitude is present, once is not enough. It's not just the number of times we offer thanks, gratitude generates so much bountiful pleasure that we can't just credit one person—we thank the Universe, too.

Giving thanks to God—or if you prefer, to the natural order of things—is a common reaction to the AV of gratitude. Deep in our psyches, we realize that all good fortune originates somewhere, and for many this means God, "from whom all blessings flow." This isn't just church-speak, this is a reference to some people's understanding of how the universe works.

Not only does gratitude move us to thank our benefactors, it compels us to share our good fortune. Generosity is a natural spin-off. When we are deeply grateful, we become eager to offer whatever it is we have. And that is infinitely easier when we have made the deliberate choice to focus on the abundance of life.

In addition to moving us to say and give thanks, gratitude opens our hearts and our ears. It enables us to listen honestly without judgment to whatever response comes from our helpmate. A *no* response will matter less to us because we understand in our bones that we are blessed. A *yes* will only serve to confirm our belief that the world is an abundant place and that help is available, if we only ask for it.

Anytime we ask for assistance, we create a potentially stressful situation for our helpmate. It is hard to know which emotions may be triggered. Depending on her situation, your helper might feel pleased or panicked, happy or disinclined to help. Remember to direct compassion toward her, just as you direct it toward your self. The relaxed and carefree attitude you feel will create a space for authenticity and honest conversation.

Encouraged by the AV of gratitude, we say thank you—no matter the response. And, we give thanks—no matter the response. We listen with open hearts—no matter what.

## Learning the AV of Gratitude

We learn the basics of gratitude as children. When we are young we are taught that saying thank-you is the appropriate response for any act of generosity directed toward us. Neglecting to say thanks when we are little is excusable, but to forget to say thank-you when we are adults is unjustifiable. So, our elders make every effort to instill this basic lesson of civil company. But is learning to say thank-you the same as learning gratitude? Not quite.

While our elders teach us about saying thanks, most of us learn the deep lessons of the applied virtues during personal epiphanies. Gina's epiphany came at the whiteboard. Laura experienced her awakening with a snowflake.

A powerhouse of a boss, Laura was able to accomplish great things with her very small staff. Part of her approach to driving her team, however, was to focus on the negative. Laura possessed a scarcity mentality and as a result perceived only what was missing or wrong. Her sharp analytical skills helped her zero in on the mistakes and problems made by her staff and peers. After a while it became painfully clear to her that this negative approach did nothing to inspire her team, nor did it nourish her with the optimistic energy she really craved.

One snowy midwestern day as we sat in a conference room, I realized that the only thing that Laura lacked was gratitude for what she had. As I listened to her talk, I gazed out the window. It was one of those stunningly beautiful days when there was so much light bouncing off the snow that it hurt to look for long. It was too good an opportunity to miss. I told Laura to grab her coat and within a few minutes we were outside.

Standing in the snow in her dress shoes, Laura was just uncomfortable enough to want to go back inside. She was also more than a little worried that someone from upper management might see her and wonder if she had lost her mind. I recognized these complaints as ego-based. My intuition told me that Laura had been too comfortable in her old habits and that her worry about the opinion of others (fear of shame) was working against her. After a while, when she realized I wasn't going to let her go back inside, she decided to play along. I asked her to look around and tell me what she saw.

She raised her eyes and then slowly lowered them. Laura had followed the descent of a single snowflake to her coat sleeve. She stared at it for a long while—it was way too cold for it to melt. When she finally looked up again, I saw that everything about her had changed. Her face beamed with joy.

Laura had rediscovered gratitude. Through that one snowflake, a new reality had been revealed. Laura finally perceived the beauty and abundance that was all around her. She also understood that she had a choice: She could complain about the snow in her expensive pumps or she could behold the beauty and perfection that transcended the cold. What's more, Laura finally grasped that she could make the same choice back inside in her warm and dry office. She could choose to see only what was wrong or she could see beyond all that to the talented team that she had recruited.

**TRY THIS**   GENERATE GRATITUDE

Here are some ways to make gratitude a part of your day.

◆ Keep a Gratitude Journal. Oprah Winfrey advocated this as an ongo-
  ing practice a few years ago on her television show. Every day record
  at least five things, people, events, and situations for which you are
  grateful.

◆ Meditate on gratitude. With each new meditation, ask yourself a
  question such as, "When was the last time I felt gratitude?" And
  "How can I bring the joy of gratitude into my life every day?" Or
  "What would my life be like if I lived and acted from gratitude?"

◆ Choose to be aware of your blessings. Once a day, identify someone
  for whom you are grateful. Pay attention to all they do for you and
  how they impact your life. Record your thoughts in your journal.

◆ Take a walk. Pay particular attention to the innocuous elements of
  your neighborhood: sidewalks, mailboxes, curbs, parking signs, and
  trash cans. Ask yourself, "How can I be grateful for these mundane
  blessings?"

◆ Have a party. Invite friends and family over and ask them to bring
  a list of their own blessings. Ask each person to share their list and
  then toast each other in celebration of the abundance of life.

## Changing Perceptions with the AV of Gratitude

Like all of the applied virtues, gratitude has the potential to
change our lives—if we let it. Gratitude sheds light on the
darkness and reveals a different, more accurate existence. It
causes the gaps to narrow, the empty emotional spaces to diminish and our needs to become surmountable. It gives us
back our smiles.

   Even in the depth of our need, we can rediscover gratitude.
When we do, our relationships and circumstances are put into
perspective. Nothing seems as it was. Melody Beattie, author
of *The Language of Letting Go*, writes, "Gratitude unlocks the

fullness of life. It turns what we have into enough, and more. It turns denial into acceptance, chaos into order, confusion into clarity. It turns problems into gifts, failures into success, the unexpected into perfect timing, and mistakes into important events. Gratitude makes sense of our past, brings peace for today and creates a vision for tomorrow." Gratitude does all this.

Even those who experience the worst that life has to offer know the power of gratitude to help them escape their pain, survive their trials, and thrive in a new life. Yvonne had a terrifying childhood filled with abuse, neglect, and drugs. Yet every day, she tells me, she remains thankful for her life. She knows that every past moment of pain and anguish has influenced who she is today. I can attest that she is a remarkable woman. As hard as it is to believe, and as difficult as it is to rein in our anger and disgust at such criminal behavior, Yvonne feels compassion for her tormentors.

I marvel at her resilience, as well as her ability to view the crimes against her as gifts—as blessings. If she can perceive the conditions of her life differently, we can do the same with our own.

## The Choice: The AV of Gratitude

When Yvonne first told me the details of how she had been used as a child, I was horrified. It is hard to believe that anyone could have survived her experiences, let alone grown into a well-adjusted adult.

I asked her how she came through it all. She replied that at eighteen, after living on her own for two years, she realized she needed help. She put herself into therapy. During these sessions, she understood that all that had happened to her could be interpreted differently, not only as a painful chapter, but as a gift. She discovered that, each and every day, she would have to make a purposeful decision to be grateful. Gratitude showed her how to transform her life into an abundant reality.

Yvonne is an extraordinarily wise woman. As a young adult, she understood she could easily allow her past to become the nightmares of her present and future. No one would have blamed her if she had decided to hold onto the pain and misery. This would have been the easy way out. But she wanted a life where the power of those who abused her would be diminished. She wanted to love, not dread, every new day. Rather than remaining reactive to the past, she made the hard choice to be proactive, to appreciate deeply the blessings of each new day.

This woman, who lived through a life most of us couldn't even imagine, made a deliberate choice to see her experiences not only for what they were, but for what they are now. Gratitude has shown her a new reality and given her a new life.

## TRY THIS   WHO IS YOUR INSPIRATION?

Who inspires you to be grateful?

♦ Reflect on your own history. Consider those times when life was rough. Ask yourself, "How am I grateful for that experience?"

♦ Talk to someone much older or younger than yourself. Ask them to tell you what they feel most grateful for. See what you can learn from them and their experiences. How can they inspire you?

♦ Look for stories of those who have survived and thrived. For example, former Vice President Al Gore suffered a humiliating defeat in his run for the presidency. Yet he has risen beyond his failure and found a new purpose: educating the world on the risks of global warming. Every day, he asks for help to save our planet.

## Yes or No?

Gratitude shifts our perceptions. It frees us to see life differently. We already know that if you carry a deep appreciation for all that you have been given, then a positive response—yes, I will help you—will be perceived as another blessing. And if this same gratitude is at home in your heart, then a negative response—no, I cannot help you—will be perceived as a gift, too.

You might ask, how can this be? How can a no be viewed so positively? Each mayday call creates the possibility of new connection and new relationships. This means that every time someone transmits a mayday signal, a new conversation is instantaneously begun. Because you asked, regardless of the answer, you altered the relationship. Your question has changed the future.

If your helpmate agrees to lend a hand, you now have a new opportunity to learn, to grow, and to share life for a while. A no still affords you future opportunities for intimacy and connection. It may manifest as a chance for you to get a clearer and more accurate picture of your relationship. For example, you may have assumed that the bond between you and your helpmate was stable enough to handle a mayday cry. Because you asked, you shed a light on an interpersonal connection that may not be as strong or as healthy as you might have thought. Be grateful. This new information can be used to help both of you create a better, stronger relationship.

A negative response may also provide you with insight to the challenges faced by your helpmate. It just may be that he is overwhelmed himself. His rejection of your appeal may be an indication that he has a mayday call of his own to make. This again, is another chance for you to explore and deepen your bond.

Recently, I called upon my neighbor, Sarah, to watch my dog for the afternoon. She had willingly done so in the past and I believed she even enjoyed having my little furball for company. But this time, things were different. As I explained my plight, I saw that she looked tired and a bit worn out. I guessed that I might have relied on her once too often or that her current problems were much greater than mine. I actually felt relieved when Sarah said no. Rather than demanding, "Why can't you help me?" I inquired, "What's going on?" We spent the next few minutes talking about her and her life. This new conversation deepened our friendship and tacitly reassured her that I valued our relationship too much to abuse her generosity. Sarah's negative response to my mayday cry was a blessing to us both.

By the way, because I was acting with faith, I knew my need would eventually be met—and it was. Later that day, I met a young man who was looking for customers for his brand new dog walking service! I hired him on the spot!

A refusal can also show us which relationships have run their course. I decided to let go of just such a friendship a few years ago. Whenever Isabelle and I got together for dinner or drinks, we invariably ended up talking about what was happening in her life. I believe she honestly valued my friendship, but I also think she valued my coaching talents more. Eventually, there came a time when I needed support myself. I asked her to help me. My simple request sent this woman off on a rant that brought up many of the issues that we had been hiding from ourselves. I was thankful that I had asked, and that she had said no, because I was shown a reality that I had chosen to ignore. Our relationship was not healthy—for either of us. I might not ever have seen this had I decided to keep my needs to myself. This new perspective allowed me to let go and to make room for new and more satisfying friendships.

## Gratitude and the Fears

Most people will tell you that they don't ask for help because they don't want to experience rejection. This may be true, but at least as many fear being seen as weak or exposed. Possessing gratitude means that one has seen and acknowledged what is and has chosen to disregard what may be missing. Fear, the voice of the ego, whispers repeatedly that asking for help telegraphs powerlessness, a position of want and lack. It's as though we see a neon sign flashing above our heads that advertises, "I'm weak! Take advantage of me!"

A deliberate focus on the gifts you have been given keeps you strong and resolved. Asking for help will no longer be a mark of vulnerability, but a declaration of your worth as an individual. Your words and behaviors will reflect the joy you feel inside. All of this enables you to ask confidently for what you need. Your mayday signal will reflect that self-assurance.

Instead of being concerned that your request will be interpreted as a sign of weakness, you will feel nothing of the kind. Instead of being ashamed that you lack something in your life, you will recognize and accept that you cannot do or have it all. Instead of worrying whether you will be rejected, you will know with certainty that, even if this person says no, assistance will arrive somehow, someway.

Gratitude not only liberates you from your fear, but it frees your helpmate too. As long as you feel blessed, he or she will naturally be more comfortable responding to your request for aid. Instead of reacting to a perceived weakness with pity, she will more likely respond to your strength with compassion—a willingness to share and alleviate your pain.

## Kristi's Story

Everyone thought she was crazy. Here she was a grown woman, a recently retired audiologist, moving in with her elderly parents. But Kristi didn't care what everyone else thought. She knew this was the right move for her.

As she approached her retirement date, Kristi was unsure about her future. She had saved enough money to live on, but Kristi knew that she would have to find a part-time job to supplement her savings. Her plan was to travel the world for a year and then settle down in a small town somewhere. So, she sold her house and put the profits in her retirement fund. Buying a new home didn't make sense to her if she was going to be traveling the world, and renting an apartment that would remain empty much of the year seemed like another waste of her hard-earned dollars. So, Kristi approached her parents and asked them if they would mind if she moved in with them.

Cautious in her request, Kristi knew that her parents valued their privacy and enjoyed their empty-nest life. She made certain her parents understood that she would pay rent and contribute to all the bills, and that she would give them as much time to themselves as they needed. As Kristi broached the idea with her parents, she silently reminded herself how lucky she was to have this chance. Not everyone is able to quit work young and spend a year on a personal sabbatical. She knew that no matter their response, everything would be fine.

Her parents agreed and she moved into the guestroom. As time went on, Kristi started to receive calls from her two brothers. Evan and Connor both thought Kristi was a little crazy to have moved back home. "How can she deal with their eccentricities? How can she stand it?" they wondered. Kristi quickly tired of their comments. She told them, "I am so lucky to be here, even if it isn't perfect. Plus, I know we aren't going to have mom and dad around forever, so I am going to cherish every moment I can." That shut them up.

Kristi lived her life from the applied virtue of gratitude. She sincerely appreciated her parents' sacrifice. She valued her unusual situation for what it offered her: flexibility, a chance to take the trip of a lifetime, and time to spend with those she loved. Gratitude shifted her focus away from the "eccentricities" of a long-married couple. Instead, she saw a different, more true, reality. She was blessed to have this opportunity. Nothing else mattered, certainly not her parents' peculiarities.

The applied virtue of gratitude reveals what we cannot see as long as we believe the lies told by our fears. We remain blind to all the good that is right in front of us. When we regain our sight, we finally perceive how wonderful life already is.

# STEP 6

# LISTEN DIFFERENTLY

> There was a definite process by which one made
> people into friends, and it involved talking to them
> and listening to them for hours at a time.
> *Dame Rebecca West*

You've prepared, you've empowered yourself, and you've voiced your mayday call. Supported by self-compassion, faith, and gratitude, all you can do now is listen.

## Step 6: Listen Differently

The two anchoring principles of the *Mayday!* process both deal with emotions. The first is that emotions drive action and language. The second is that powerful emotional states are required to overcome our fear of asking for help. It's not a surprise then, that listening differently requires us to attend to the hidden emotional messages being conveyed. Step 6 is no longer about you and your needs. This step requires you to focus on your helpmate.

Consider what you do when you direct your mayday call to a specific individual. You ask him to step into your life and give of his talents and skills to make your existence better. If he agrees, your helpmate sacrifices something, even if it is just energy, to meet your need. The very least you can do is to listen to, and not just hear, what he has to say.

## The Enchantment of Listening

Being listened to is enchanting. When we know someone is attending to us, we fall under a spell that changes the future, turning a gray day to one filled with light. And like all magic, it is too rare a thing.

For me, the hardest thing to learn to do as a coach was to listen. An occasional (some say frequent) know-it-all, I struggled to keep my mouth shut in those early coaching years. I chastised myself whenever I decided I knew the answer—what the client should do—rather than allowing the client to discover it herself. And I became frustrated every time I found myself "telling" a client something rather than asking a question. It became clear early on that I had to change in order to effectively serve my clients.

My schooling began by watching how others reacted when someone actually listened to them. Years ago, my friend Dean and I met for lunch at a trendy restaurant. Though the venue was perfect, our server was downright rude. Rather than complain to management, Dean did something surprising. When the waitress returned, he asked a question, "It's very busy in here today. Are you responsible for this whole section?" Dean listened closely to her response. Then, he asked her another question, "How long have you worked here?" He listened again as she explained that she had been a server there for the past ten years. I could see they were making eye contact now. Another question from Dean, "Really, that long? What's the best part of your job?" With this, the server started to smile, her shoulders lowered a bit and her face became more animated. No longer grumpy and rude, she was now absolutely charming.

Dean changed the dynamics of our situation simply by asking questions and listening to the answers. This was a revelation to me. By the time she had taken our orders, our server was a different woman. After she left the table, I asked, "Was that deliberate on your part? Did you know that you could change her attitude just by asking questions and listening to her?" Dean replied, "I remember what it was like to wait tables. Customers act as though waiters are necessary nuisances. I like to make sure that every server is seen and heard by me."

More than anything else, people want to be seen and to be heard. Listening is magical precisely because it accomplishes both. When someone listens to us with sincere intent, we feel acknowledged and recognized. Any isolation we suffer disappears and in its place is set a feeling of belonging.

Deafness, some believe, is the most isolating of handicaps. None of us would choose to be deaf, of course, yet we isolate ourselves every day when we neglect to listen to each other. Listening, really listening, is a perfect way to reduce our feelings of separateness and regain more of the connectedness that we might have lost.

This experience in the restaurant spurred me to learn to listen even more. I took advantage of every chance I could. I was even able to listen to Kevin, a man who, when nervous, talked nonstop. His co-workers had complained to me more than once about how his explanations went on, seemingly without end. My experiences with Kevin were no different. In the first few months of our coaching sessions, I was barely able to get a word in, let alone ask any questions. I thought about ending the coaching relationship a couple of times because we didn't seem to be getting anywhere. Instead, my heart told me to hold on and listen just a little longer. When I noticed frustration or impatience within me, I inhaled deeply and listened some more. I challenged myself to remain quiet.

I'm thankful I did. Kevin slowly started to change his communication patterns. I cannot be certain what triggered it, but my assessment is that Kevin just needed to be heard. Perhaps when he received focused listening from a coach, he didn't need to keep talking. At this point our coaching conversations really took off.

Kevin isn't alone in wanting to be heard. Many people, especially those at the highest level of an organization, have no one to talk to. They don't get to experience the acknowledgement, recognition, and connection that comes when one is truly heard.

Your potential helpmate has listened closely to your request. If you've relied on self-compassion, faith, and gratitude, then she's sure to have heard it clearly. Now, it is equally important to listen as closely to the response to our cry for help.

## TRY THIS    PRACTICE LISTENING

A number of techniques can help you practice listening. Here are a few:

♦ Listen to someone you might normally neglect to converse with, like a waiter or a bank teller. Make eye contact. (Though we hear with our ears, our eyes tell the speaker we are listening to every word.) Use complete inquiries and not just statements that are delivered like questions. For example, say, "How do you deal with the intensity of your job?" Avoid saying, "Your job is pretty intense, huh?" The former is a bit more formal, but it is also an overt invitation to conversation. The latter simply requires a yes or no response. It doesn't engender conversation. Remember to pause after you pose a question. No matter how tempted you are, slow down, breathe, and take a break after your question. Give the person time to respond.

♦ Observe how others listen. Notice those who seem to listen well, who ask great questions, and who keep the conversation going without directing attention to themselves. See what you can learn from them.

♦ Ask a friend, spouse, or partner to sit opposite you. Sit quietly for five minutes without saying a word. Notice what you can pick up about their body language and their emotional state as you do this. Pay attention to what you might convey as well.

♦ Join an improv class if there is one in your area. Learn from the pros about listening. Those improv performers who are really good are the ones who listen the best. An improv class has plenty of simple and hilarious activities that will teach you the finer points of listening. You will learn how to pick up on messages that are simultaneously subtle and obvious.

♦ Focus your attention on the person you are listening to. Challenge yourself to see how many questions you can ask during your conversation. See how often you can redirect questions intended for you.

## Hearing and Listening

When we listen, we involve our bodies, minds, and emotions. Think back to your early biology lessons, the ones where you learned about the internal structures that made hearing possible. Our ears are fascinating little machines, constantly absorbing the vibrations of sound and transmitting them back to the inner reaches of our brains. Once there, those vibrations get translated into meaningful impulses. We hear—a reflexive, physiological act. Unless our ears are covered, we cannot stop from hearing.

Hearing is not the same as listening, however. Every frustrated parent of a rebellious teenager knows that we hear, but we may not always listen. Julio Olalla, founder of the Newfield Network, has an interesting way of reinforcing the distinction between the two. He might say, "What I listened is that you . . ." Julio's awkward phrasing is intended to drive home the fact that what we hear and what we listen can be very different things.

Unlike hearing, listening is a deliberate act. We must selectively attune to a message to truly listen to it. After we have vocalized our plea for help, we must be sure to not only hear our helpmate's answer but to listen to it.

## Listening Differently

On the surface, what we listen for is a yes or no response to our requests for help. But to listen differently, we must listen for more.

A lot happens in every conversation between two people.

♦ Each person uses a complicated and ancient language to convey her position and to generate questions. This complexity of language can lead to a great deal of misunderstanding.

♦ Each person relies on a set of internal perceptions that spring from previously held interpretations. Though each interpretation is valid, there is no way to ensure that the other person holds the same understanding.

♦ The success of our conversation also depends on the silent messages we convey with our bodies. No matter how well-versed we are in the use of spoken language, we must be equally expert in how we use our physical beings.

♦ Emotions fly to and fro during each conversation. You already know about fear, sympathy, hope, and appreciation, not to mention the pumped-up emotions of compassion, faith, and gratitude. During any request you make, you might find yourself in one or all of these emotional states.

No wonder we experience communication breakdowns! All of these thoughts, messages and emotions take place at once. And, that's only on your side of the table! You can assume that your helpmate is experiencing a similar kind of organized chaos. Most of us will admit to being poor listeners. But think of how complex the skill really is. Perhaps you should exercise a little self-compassion and cut yourself a little slack in this regard. After all, you are able to achieve a decent level of communication with other people, despite all this confusion.

That said, a truly skilled listener attunes to the entire person, including his words, how he uses his body, and the emotions at play. This holistic listening is what I refer to as listening differently.

To listen differently, direct your attention to how your helpmate responds. What words does she use? What is the tone of her voice? How fast does she speak? What can you surmise from the language or the choice of words she uses?

Shift your attention to her physical being. Look for all the usual clues: eye contact, nervous habits, posture, and the pace of her breathing. Is your helper out of breath or does she seem a bit unfocused? You might want to give her a moment or two to get settled before you continue. As you become more adept at listening, you will notice how your helper's body interacts with your own. Are the two of you moving in concert? Do your gestures mirror one another's? Is there a sensation that you are acting jointly? If you answer yes, then that's a hopeful sign that she is open to helping you.

As you observe the physical, see what you can surmise about the emotions of your helper. Is she calm or now suddenly nervous? Does her body language indicate confidence in her ability to help you or does she appear uncertain? Is she surprised that you need assistance or that you selected her to help you? Does she appear willing or does she seem reticent?

A good friend of mine, Greg, helps me care for my home. I am not skilled at doing some tasks, like tiling a backsplash or hanging a new door. He is always willing to help. Bless his heart, Greg has a hard time saying no. Because of his tendency to say yes, I make it a point to observe his use of language, his physical response, and his emotional attachment to my mayday calls. I listen differently so I can detect doubt, impatience, or uncertainty.

Your helpmate answers you with more than just words. Pay attention to the entire message, not just what you physically hear with your ears. Listening to the body, language, and emotions will help you discern any disconnects that might exist.

## Listening for the Disconnect

Listening differently also means listening beyond the yes or no response. It means attuning to the match between the verbal response and the emotion embedded in the background. As Julio would say, do you "listen to" a welcoming yes, or one filled with trepidation? Is it a fearful no, or one that is grounded in optimism? *This kind of listening protects both parties from feeling resentful and confused. Listening differently keeps us from accepting a yes that is actually a covert no, or from accepting a no that could easily become a yes.*

Differentiate between what is said and the underlying and unspoken intention. Ask yourself, "Is there a disconnect between what she is saying and how she is acting?" If your helpmate's body, language, and emotions seem out of alignment with each other, then a disconnect exists. For example, if my friend Greg responds, "Sure, I'll help you out," but his emotional presence seems strained or his body appears suddenly tense, there's a good chance he doesn't quite mean what he says. This doesn't mean he is being untruthful or duplicitous; the disconnect may simply indicate an inner uncertainty. I will not ignore what Greg is not saying! Instead, I will take the mismatch as an opportunity for additional conversation and inquiry.

Respect your helpmate and ask her what she's really feeling. We all know someone who habitually says yes to any request, like my friend Greg. There are also those who reflexively say no. By politely inquiring about and confirming their intent, you show that you are willing to protect their interests as well as your own.

I learned this very lesson when I demanded that my boyfriend care for me following my surgery. You may remember that he agreed, and that I did notice a clear disconnect between his words and his emotions. I heard the hesitation in his voice. I was hurt a little by it, but I was too filled with fear to care what he was feeling. I chose to ignore it, even though it was obvious he didn't want to or wasn't able to fulfill my request. The last thing any of us want is for someone to say yes when they really mean to say no.

How do you make sure that the yes means a yes? Try these approaches:

- ♦ I think I heard some hesitation in your voice. Are you certain you can help me?

- ♦ I would hate to have this request interfere with our friendship. I want to make sure you are sure you can do this for me. Can you?

- ♦ What are you thinking? I want to understand any concerns you might have.

- ♦ I appreciate your help. I want to make sure that my needs don't interfere with your own. Is there anything that you would like us to be careful of as we work on this together?

We also don't want someone to say no, especially when she would really like to help but may not know how. If you listen differently—to body, language, and emotions—you might notice another unspoken message that says, "I don't know what I could do to help." And "I don't think I'm capable of helping you." Or even, "Are you sure you think I'm the best person to help you out?" Again, do not ignore this! As frightened and nervous as you might be, rely on your faith to see you through. Go ahead and ask. Your question will lead to a new conversation, and perhaps, to a new kind of relationship. If you don't ask for clarification, then the no stays a no. But if you do, then the no still has a chance of becoming a yes.

How can you change a no to a yes? Try to start a new conversation with these:

♦ I want to make sure that this need gets met. Are there any circumstances under which you might be able to help me? What are they?

♦ Would you be willing to help me if we could figure out how to do it without it becoming too much of a burden for you?

♦ Would you be willing and able to help me with part of what I need?

## Bob's Story

A fun workshop activity drives home the point about hidden emotional messages. Split participants into two groups: Helpers and Askers. Both groups stand and move to the center of the room. The object of the activity is for the Askers to get the Helpers to feed them the breakfast or lunch that has been provided. Arrange for the food—nothing too sloppy—and bibs (large trash bags) so their clothing is protected.

Askers are taken to one side of the room and instructed to ask for help being fed. The Helpers are taken to the other side and quietly told to agree to help one Asker, but only after rejecting at least one person's request. Once both groups understand their instructions, they are brought to the center of the room. The activity begins.

As you can imagine, participants respond in various ways. There is a lot of laughter and a willingness to play along. What is revealing is how each Asker reacts when their request is rejected. Some are taken aback, surprised that a co-worker would say no to them. Others are indifferent and move on to the next Helper to see if they will agree. Very few will ask the same person twice.

One person who did was Bob. He didn't bat an eye when his request was turned down by Cathy, one of his peers. Instead, he became curious and he began to ask her questions, "Why won't you help me? And "Is it because you want to help someone else? Or, is it because you worry about helping me in particular?" Cathy replied that neither of those reasons was relevant. Her answer made him even more curious, so he tried another tack. He tried buttering her up, telling her that because she was a mother of an infant daughter, he figured she would be expert at feeding people. "I want only the best to feed me," he added. She rolled her eyes at the obvious flattery, but she was impressed with his perseverance. Within a few minutes he had her laughing so hard, she agreed to feed him his breakfast.

Bob understood that a no can become a yes, but only after a new conversation begins. He didn't take the rejection to heart and he used his own sense of humor to relax his chosen Helper. And Cathy wanted to help him, and not just because of the obvious flattery. She sincerely appreciated his inquiring approach.

People are naturally generous. This innate kindness rests just below the surface of all the other emotions we feel during a day. As soon as a mayday cry goes out and is listened to, that generosity of heart breaks through. When it does, you will find that people are eager to help.

We all experience excitement when given a chance to contribute and make a difference in this world. When someone reaches out from a place of need, he gives us permission to reveal energy that is normally buried within. Holding back, doing it on our own cheats others of an opportunity to shine. Our appeals for aid set in motion a series of interactions and conversations that not only change us, they move the world toward greater connection and understanding.

## TRY THIS    LISTENING FOR THE DISCONNECT

This skill can be learned easily, all it takes is deliberate observation and practice. Try these approaches to improve your understanding of the disconnect between the spoken words and our emotional state.

♦ Watch children closely. At a certain young age, they begin to fib. Adults see through most of these lies, but we rarely examine how we can tell the child is fibbing. What is it about the child that doesn't match with the words he uses? Observe his eye contact, his posture. What indicates that a lie is in progress?

♦ Make a Disconnect Jar. With a good friend or spouse, agree that anytime one of you notices a disconnect between words, action, and emotions, you will mention it. The person who exhibited the disconnect must donate a dollar to the Disconnect Jar. At the end of the month, empty the jar and treat yourselves to coffee (a few disconnects), lunch (a few more disconnects), or dinner (many, many disconnects).

♦ Pay attention to your own disconnects. Do you agree to things that you really don't want to do? Do you want to say yes, but don't really know how? If you are willing, journal about these situations. Pull as much learning as you can from each experience.

# STEP 7

# SAY THANKS

∎∎∎ ▬ ▬ ▬ ∎∎∎

Give thanks for a little and you will find a lot.
*The Hausa of Nigeria*

Congratulations! You've reached the final step in the *Mayday!* process! Look at all you've learned. You now understand the temporary power that fear has over you and the lies that it tells. You realize the importance of getting clear on what you need, and at the same time, you know it is equally important to be open to other suggestions. The magic embedded in the applied virtues of self-compassion, faith, and gratitude have seen you through. These "emotions on steroids" have changed your physical presence and your words, so your mayday calls become strong, with dignity and self-respect. Along the way, you picked up some practical tips on who, when, and how to ask. Listening differently, you have heard the hidden emotional messages underlying your helpmate's response. The final step, of course, is to say thank-you.

## Step 7: Say Thanks

Just as you learned to be clear in your requests for assistance, it's equally important to be obvious in your gratitude. Say thank-you openly and loud enough so your partner can hear.

If you receive a negative response to your mayday call, be especially certain your partner knows you accept the refusal. Express your disappointment, but remember this is not the time to lay on the guilt (not that there is ever a good time). Forcing others to feel guilty is an attempt to shift responsibility. Not only is this an awful thing to do, it doesn't serve you in the long run. You are responsible for your own life. Asking for and receiving help does not remove accountability from your shoulders to someone else's. It always remains your own.

If you hear and listen to a no, offer your thanks for the time your helpmate spent and his willingness to listen. Smile, if you can. Make it easy on your friend. Show him you know and believe that everything will turn out as it should. This same person may be in your life for quite a while. Someday you may have to come back and ask for something else. Or just as important, your friend may need to come to you with a request of his own. Now is a great time to set a precedent of loving and respectful behavior in your mutual mayday calls.

Even if the answer is "Yes, I will help you," some of us are still unskilled when it comes to saying thank-you. Personally, I know I've overdone it a few times. I'm so grateful for the yes response that I end up gushing. There isn't anything wrong with a good gush every now and then, but going overboard can be a bit embarrassing and unnecessary. It can also make your helpmate feel awkward. With practice, you can find a balance between the size of the favor and your level of gratitude. Be authentic. Being real goes a long way. Sometimes all it takes is a sincere look into your helper's eyes and a firm handshake.

Another way in which we flub our thanks is when we don't
say it often enough. To avoid this, use the Three Thanks rule.
Make it a practice of expressing your gratitude three times.
First, say thank-you when the agreement for help is struck.
Second, say thanks when the need has been met. And, third,
say thanks the next time you see your helpmate. It's not necessary to make a big production out of it, but it is important
to follow through. We have all been in situations where we've
been thanked the first time, but not the second. As an occasional helper, twice strikes me as inadequate for the really big
favors. A third thank-you indicates that you haven't forgotten the sacrifice that was made.

Archie does a lot for his children. Though grown, they
still rely on him for financial support. This can be somewhat
taxing, but Archie enjoys being generous with his time. One
son, however, when asking for help, says thanks only twice.
He makes it a point of telling his father how much he loves
him when he agrees to a request. And, he is openly grateful
when he receives the favor. But then Archie never hears another word from him about it. Archie worries that he might
be too stingy in his attitude, when it's really his son who is
too miserly with his gratitude. If, the next time they get together, Archie's son would only offer him a handshake and
say, "Thanks again, Dad," I'm sure he'd feel much better.
That third thank-you lets your benefactor know your appreciation survives beyond the duration of the favor or help.

**TRY THIS    THANK-YOU PRACTICE**

♦ Practice saying thank-you one day a week. Make sure that the subject of your gratitude hears and understands your thank-you.

♦ Notice how many times you are thanked in a week. Avoid making
judgments if you don't receive a thank-you, but openly acknowledge
the gratitude you receive.

## The Law of Reciprocity Revisited

The Law of Reciprocity, a feeling that we must pay in kind for acts of generosity, creates a kind of domino effect within our relationships. When we hear that positive response, a yes, we experience a rush of gratitude. In turn, this profound appreciation taps into our own personal generosity. We respond by wanting to give back. This cascade makes us want to say, "If I can do anything for you, please let me know."

The Law of Reciprocity will always kick in just as you ask for a step up. It acts as a safety valve that prevents us from abusing the generosity of others. When that happens, ask yourself, "How much has my helpmate lost by doing this for me; what have they sacrificed?" If you do not judge it to be much, be sure to answer the question again, this time from the helpmate's perspective. You might not think it was a big deal having someone come bail you out of jail, but perhaps she did!

Then ask yourself, "How often have I asked for help from this person?" If your intuition tells you it has been too often, go back to your list of potential helpmates and select another name.

Just remember that a transactional approach of give-and-take isn't always necessary. Let go of counting favors and trust your helpmates. Have faith that all will balance in the end.

## Payback Time

Let's assume you have made a substantial request—perhaps to borrow a large sum of money—which may make you feel as though you owe your helper "big time." Do both you and your helpmate a favor: Bring up the uncomfortable conversation about repayment. Be just as deliberate about this as you were in making the request for help. Asking for a loan can cause great interpersonal damage. Make it your responsibility to protect the relationship.

From the helper's viewpoint, it's scary to take on the role of personal banker and loan money; there are lots of uneasy questions about when and if it will ever be repaid. Be proactive: Answer these awkward questions before she has time to ask them.

Some helpmates refuse to charge interest for loans, others insist on it. Don't allow the generosity of your benefactor to get in the way of a plan to pay it all back. Instead, add a little extra to each payment. If payment is refused, then treat for dinner now and then. Demonstrate your gratitude.

If the help is harder to quantify, say emotional support during a difficult time, then have fun with your repayment plan. Let your creativity go and see if you can't come up with some delightful ways to reciprocate. Offer to babysit or spring for a restaurant or bookstore gift certificate. Take your benefactor to a ball game or bring over a six-pack of his favorite beer. Let generosity bloom and see how many different ways you can say thanks.

Now, at the end of the *Mayday!* process, you have been the recipient of great gifts of affection, intimacy, love, and flow. Give back when you can, and always say thank-you.

## CONCLUSION

# MAYDAY, MAY DAY

We all need assistance. Those who sustain others
themselves want to be sustained.
*Maurice Hulst*

Asking for help is an unconventional, counterintuitive approach to getting our needs met. How ironic. We are social animals who can literally die without the support of others. We require connection, attention, and intimacy to remain whole and healthy, yet we deny, day after day, our need for one another. We choose to pretend that we can get by, dealing with every issue and meeting every need by ourselves.

Asking for help has become a shameful signal of weakness and vulnerability. This has been accomplished through the lies and half-truths told by our fears of surrender, separation, and shame. Caught in the riptide of these fears, we tumble about, sometimes ending up more confused and frightened than when we started.

Each year swimmers die from being caught in rip currents. Typically, the trapped person expends so much energy fighting his way out of the riptide that he drowns. Experts now say that the best way to survive one of these dangerous currents is to simply float along with it until you find yourself parallel to the shore. When you reach that point, you can safely and more easily swim back to safety. This is another wonderful example that letting go and surrendering to the tide of life is what will save us.

The way out of the riptide of fear is through three powerful emotional states of self-compassion, faith, and gratitude. When we apply the virtues, a new reality is established based on hidden truths: We deserve, we are cared for, we are blessed. When we accept these truths, our perception changes. We see what we had been missing all along: that asking for help is a declaration of our self-worth, a bold belief in the connection of all things, and another blessing in a long line of blessings.

With new eyes, we see the possibility of a life of help, balance, growth, flow and connection. Everything that had been hidden from us is revealed in this new reality. Where we thought we were alone, we find helpmates eager to assist us. Where we thought there was scarcity, we now see abundance. Where we thought we had to fight and struggle, we now see that letting go is much more effective.

## The Mayday! Process

Crying Mayday! no longer has to be seen as a sign of desperation and hopelessness. Now, it can be seen for what it truly is, a simple, everyday request for help.

To make certain your mayday signals are transmitted with strength and clarity, you need apply only seven simple steps.

1. Name the Need

2. Give Yourself a Break

3. Take a Leap

4. Ask!

5. Be Grateful

6. Listen Differently

7. Say Thanks

If seven steps are difficult for you to remember, then remember only three:

1. Give Yourself a Break

2. Take a Leap

3. Be Grateful

The applied virtues of self-compassion, faith, and gratitude are all the support you truly need to make your request, but if you find yourself unable to focus on three, then remember only one:

1. Be Grateful

The applied virtue of gratitude makes possible the virtues of self-compassion and faith. In times of need remember that the AV of gratitude "is the parent of all others." Possessed by gratitude, your mayday calls will be supported by the abundance of your life.

## Mayday, May Day

*M'aidez* is French for "help me." Mayday has become the universal signal for help. There is still another way of seeing this word.

Centuries ago, when people lived closer to the land and to each other, when we relied on our neighbors for help on a daily basis, May Day signified celebration. May First was set aside as a time to observe the end of another winter and to formally welcome springtime. It was a day to commemorate the renewal of friendships and to see the long-missed faces that had been hidden by scarves and heavy coats. May Day was also a time to honor physical intimacy and the miracle of creation.

Each day that we ask for the help we need, each time we use our mayday signals, we give ourselves a chance to commemorate a new kind of May Day. Our calls for help have the potential to refresh us, to renew our relationships, and to generate different futures built on compassion, faith, and gratitude. Living from virtue, we have a chance to experience tight friendships, deep intimacy, strong connections, and the abundance of life. Every single one of our mayday cries can easily become *May Day* celebrations.

# RESOURCES

Here are the Riptide and Applied Virtue Matrices for easy reference. They provide simple reminders of the truth: that you are worthy and deserving of the help you seek. Rely on them when the riptide of fear takes hold.

## THE RIPTIDE MATRIX

| | The Riptide of Surrender | The Riptide of Separation | The Riptide of Shame |
|---|---|---|---|
| The Lie | All control is good and the loss of control is very bad. | You have always been alone and you are alone now. | You are flawed. You must never let anyone see your flaws or they will be repulsed by you. |
| Related Concerns | Loss of independence<br><br>Concern over the price tag for help<br><br>Fear of the unknown<br><br>Loss of control over how things are done<br><br>Loss of financial security | Risk of losing one's job<br><br>Banishment from the family or community<br><br>Fear of rejection | Concern over revealing one's weaknesses<br><br>Feeling unworthy or undeserving |
| The Truth Behind the Fear | Control is impossible and surrender can be glorious. | You are not alone. | You are worthy of help. |

# THE APPLIED VIRTUE MATRIX

| Applied Virtue | Definition | The Emotional Seed | Combined with | The Hidden Message |
|---|---|---|---|---|
| Compassion | A desire to alleviate the suffering of others | Sympathy: an understanding of another's suffering | A desire to act on behalf of someone else | Others are deserving of help |
| Self-Compassion | A desire to alleviate our own suffering | Sympathy: an understanding of our own suffering | A desire to act on one's own behalf | You are deserving of help |
| Faith | A deep belief that you will be cared for even if the outcome is unclear | Hope: an optimistic belief for the future | A leap of faith; surrender | You will be cared for; you are not alone |
| Gratitude | A profound appreciation for life's blessings | Appreciation: an understanding of the importance or value of something | Mindfulness | You are blessed! |

## Mayday! Salons

Asking for help requires us to invite others into our own lives. Many of us have had enough of doing it alone. If you choose to create a deliberate support system, like the one described in Step 4, then you might also be interested in establishing a *Mayday!* Salon. The purpose of a Salon is to deepen your learning about the process, to support one another in its implementation, and to help you track your own personal growth. Below are a few suggestions for making your Salons effective.

### Invite a Variety of Interested Parties

Talk up the *Mayday!* process. Let people know that you are learning to ask for what you need. Invite others to learn about the process. If three or more of you are implementing the process, suggest you meet to create a Salon of your own.

Deliberate support teams include those who will push us beyond our own limits. Keeping this in mind, try not to limit your membership to just your friends and buddies. Invite others who see life differently than you do. You will expand your own comfort zones and they will contribute their own perspectives and insights.

### Set Regular Meeting Days/Times

Regular meetings can become a burden on busy lives. Meetings that happen too infrequently can slowly fade away. Striking the right balance of how often, when, and where you meet may take some trial and error.

Start with monthly meetings on an evening that is best for the majority of the members. Check in every few meetings to see how the date and time is working for everyone. If it isn't, feel free to change it.

## *Select One Topic per Salon*

There are so many subjects to cover when it comes to asking for help. Take each of the major topics and make them come alive with your own stories and experiences. Here are some suggested topics:

- ◆ The benefit of interpersonal connection
- ◆ The benefit of flow
- ◆ The benefit of a life of ease, simplicity, and renewed energy
- ◆ The fear of surrender
- ◆ The fear of separation
- ◆ The fear of shame
- ◆ Other ways to define need
- ◆ Ideas to generate self-compassion
- ◆ Ideas to generate faith
- ◆ Ideas to generate gratitude
- ◆ Other tips to make asking easier
- ◆ Personal lessons on how to listen differently
- ◆ Great ideas on how to say thank-you

## Share the Responsibility of Hosting, Moderating, and Recording

Consider alternating the roles of hosts, moderators, and recorders.

*Hosts* provide the venue for the meeting.

*Moderators* help facilitate the Salons, making sure they don't veer off track or get bogged down in one person's experiences.

*Recorders* take notes that might be useful to post on a website or just share between Salon members. This role is optional and definitely not necessary to the success of your Salons.

### Structure Your Meetings

There is something to be said about consistency and predictability. Structure provides comfort and creates ritual. Both serve to keep your Salon thriving.

One structure, which at first glance seems to be overkill, applies to the use of ground rules. You may develop these as you go along, but if you can, create them in your very first Salon. That way, everyone knows what's expected. Ground rules also make it easier for moderators to do their jobs well.

Another helpful structure is to come up with your own individual way to celebrate success and your attempts at asking for help. Make them fun and meaningful.

Finally, every few months check in with the members to see how things are going. Discuss what works, and what doesn't. Make changes as you go to keep your Salon alive and growing.

# BIBLIOGRAPHY

Beattie, Melody, *The Language of Letting Go,* Center City, MN: Hazelden, 1996.

Canfield, Jack, and Mark Victor Hansen, *The Aladdin Factor,* New York: Berkley Books, 1995.

Carter-Scott, Cherie, *If Life is a Game, These Are the Rules,* Louisville, KY: Broadway Press, 1998.

Castle, Victoria, *The Trance of Scarcity,* San Francisco: Berrett-Koehler Publishers, 2007.

Choquette, Sonia, *Your Heart's Desire,* New York: Three Rivers Press, 1997.

Cooperrider, David, and Diana Whitney, *Appreciative Inquiry, A Positive Revolution in Change,* San Francisco: Berrett-Koehler Publishers, 2005.

Csikszentmihalyi, Mihaly, *Flow: The Psychology of Optimal Experience,* New York: Harper Perennial, 1991.

Dinesen, Isak, *Out of Africa,* New York: Modern Library, 1992.

Ford, Debbie, *The Dark Side of the Light Chasers,* New York: Riverhead Books, 1998.

Gray, John, *Men Are from Mars, Women Are from Venus,* New York: HarperCollins, 1993.

Hofstede, Geert, and Gert Jan Hofstede, *Cultures and Organizations: Software of the Mind,* New York: McGraw-Hill, 2004.

Jung, Carl Gustav, *Man and His Symbols,* New York: Doubleday, reprint 1969.

Keizer, Garret, *Help: The Original Human Dilemma,* New York: HarperCollins, 2004.

Lee, Harper, *To Kill a Mockingbird,* New York: Warner Books, 1998.

Luther, Martin, Definition of Faith: An excerpt from "An Introduction to St. Paul's Letter to the Romans," Luther's German Bible of 1522. Available at www.iclnet.org/pub/resources/text/wittenberg/luther/luther-faith.txt. (Accessed April 13, 2007)

Maslow, Abraham H., *Toward a Psychology of Being,* Hoboken, NJ: John Wiley & Sons, 3rd Ed., 1998.

Maslow, Abraham H., *Motivation and Personality,* New York: HarperCollins, 3rd Ed., 1987.

Meilaender, Gilbert C., *The Theory and Practice of Virtue,* Notre Dame, IN: University of Notre Dame Press, 1984.

Myss, Caroline, *Sacred Contracts, Awakening Your Divine Potential,* New York: Harmony Books, 2001.

O'Donohue, John, *Anam Cara, A Book of Celtic Wisdom,* New York: Harper Perennial, 1997.

Pieper, Josef, *The Four Cardinal Virtues,* Notre Dame, IN: University of Notre Dame Press, 1990.

Pieper, Josef, *Faith, Hope, Love,* Ft. Collins, CO: Ignatius Press, 1997.

Putnam, Robert D., *Bowling Alone,* New York: Simon & Schuster, 2000.

Shinoda Bolen, Jean, *Goddesses in Everywoman,* New York: Harper and Row, 1985.

Shinoda Bolen, Jean, *The Millionth Circle,* San Francisco: Conari Press, 1999.

Tolle, Eckhart, *The Power of Now, A Guide to Spiritual Enlightenment,* Novato, CA: New World Library, 1999.

# Index

# ABOUT THE AUTHOR

M. Nora Klaver, MA, MCC, is a master coach with twenty years of experience guiding professionals in Fortune 500 companies. She is founder and president of INQ Inc., Coaching Through Inquiry, an executive coaching firm dedicated to capitalizing on individual skills and talents within work environments. Her corporate clients include leaders from Allstate Financial, NCR Corp., Leo Burnett, StarCom MediaVest, Hitachi Consulting, and the Chicago Mercantile Exchange.

Specializing in leadership and organizational development, Ms. Klaver has observed that CEO and office assistant alike share similar aspirations and fears. All want to be seen, heard, and given a chance to contribute. She finds particular satisfaction in assisting her clients to discover their own personal sources of wisdom.

Ms. Klaver is an active member of the International Coach Federation (ICF), the Association for Spirit at Work

(ASAW) and the American Society for Training & Development (ASTD). A faculty member with the Infinity Foundation in Chicago, Ms. Klaver is certified as an ontological coach through the Newfield Network USA and as a Master Certified Coach through the ICF.

Ms. Klaver is a vibrant, entertaining speaker who delivers interactive presentations at the local, regional, and national levels. Additional information about her coaching and speaking services is available at www.mnoraklaver.com. More information about *Mayday!* can be found at www.maydaythebook.com.

Ms. Klaver lives near Chicago, Illinois. She enjoys international travel despite the fact it takes her away from her beagle, Ripley.

# About Berrett-Koehler Publishers

Berrett-Koehler is an independent publisher dedicated to an ambitious mission: Creating a World that Works for All.

We believe that to truly create a better world, action is needed at all levels—individual, organizational, and societal. At the individual level, our publications help people align their lives with their values and with their aspirations for a better world. At the organizational level, our publications promote progressive leadership and management practices, socially responsible approaches to business, and humane and effective organizations. At the societal level, our publications advance social and economic justice, shared prosperity, sustainability, and new solutions to national and global issues.

A major theme of our publications is "Opening Up New Space." They challenge conventional thinking, introduce new ideas, and foster positive change. Their common quest is changing the underlying beliefs, mindsets, and structures that keep generating the same cycles of problems, no matter who our leaders are or what improvement programs we adopt.

We strive to practice what we preach—to operate our publishing company in line with the ideas in our books. At the core of our approach is *stewardship*, which we define as a deep sense of responsibility to administer the company for the benefit of all of our "stakeholder" groups: authors, customers, employees, investors, service providers, and the communities and environment around us.

We are grateful to the thousands of readers, authors, and other friends of the company who consider themselves to be part of the "BK Community." We hope that you, too, will join us in our mission.

## A BK Life Book

This book is part of our BK Life series. BK Life books change people's lives. They help individuals improve their lives in ways that are beneficial for the families, organizations, communities, nations, and world in which they live and work. To find out more, visit www.bk-life.com.

# Be Connected

## Visit Our Website

Go to www.bkconnection.com to read exclusive previews and excerpts of new books, find detailed information on all Berrett-Koehler titles and authors, browse subject-area libraries of books, and get special discounts.

## Subscribe to Our Free E-Newsletter

Be the first to hear about new publications, special discount offers, exclusive articles, news about bestsellers, and more! Get on the list for our free e-newsletter by going to www.bkconnection.com.

## Get Quantity Discounts

Berrett-Koehler books are available at quantity discounts for orders of ten or more copies. Please call us toll-free at (800) 929-2929 or email us at bkp.orders@aidcvt.com.

## Host a Reading Group

For tips on how to form and carry on a book reading group in your workplace or community, see our website at www.bkconnection.com.

## Join the BK Community

Thousands of readers of our books have become part of the "BK Community" by participating in events featuring our authors, reviewing draft manuscripts of forthcoming books, spreading the word about their favorite books, and supporting our publishing program in other ways. If you would like to join the BK Community, please contact us at bkcommunity@bkpub.com.